Healthy Wealth
in Families

Healthy Wealth in Families

✦

Sharing Prosperity Happiness and Purpose

Introducing *Relational Estate Planning*

Gerald Le Van

iUniverse, Inc.

New York Lincoln Shanghai

Healthy Wealth in Families
Sharing Prosperity Happiness and Purpose

Copyright © 2007 by Gerald Le Van

All rights reserved. No part of this book may be used or reproduced by any means, graphic, electronic, or mechanical, including photocopying, recording, taping or by any information storage retrieval system without the written permission of the publisher except in the case of brief quotations embodied in critical articles and reviews.

iUniverse books may be ordered through booksellers or by contacting:

iUniverse
2021 Pine Lake Road, Suite 100
Lincoln, NE 68512
www.iuniverse.com
1-800-Authors (1-800-288-4677)

The information, ideas, and suggestions in this book are not intended to render legal advice. Before following any suggestions contained in this book, you should consult your personal attorney. Neither the author nor the publisher shall be liable or responsible for any loss or damage allegedly arising as a consequence of your use or application of any information or suggestions in this book.

ISBN: 978-0-595-44317-8 (pbk)
ISBN: 978-0-595-88647-0 (ebk)

Printed in the United States of America

For my friends

Ralph E. Brumley

wise and kind mentor

and

Nancy A. Walker

longtime loyal associate

deepest gratitude to both of you.

Contents

About This Book ...

Inevitably, shared wealth will have a profound effect on family relationships. Families who are "joined at the wallet" encounter rare opportunities and dark hazards. Gerald Le Van's new book, "Healthy Wealth in Families" offers guideposts and warning signs to families searching for happiness and purpose in the midst of their prosperity.

A wealthy family's "relational estate" is that complex mix of genes, history, heritage, and webs of relationships that connect them across generations. Its relational estate is a wealthy family's most valuable non-financial asset ... yet it is priceless.

Traditional advice to wealthy families focuses on wealth management, wealth transfer and tax avoidance. Scant attention is paid to the impact of this financial advice on the family's relational estate. Yet, their relational estate is where wealthy families *live*. Le Van introduces "relational estate planning", new techniques that coordinate traditional financial advice with family needs and circumstances.

Le Van cautions that wealthy families must assume responsibility for their own relational estate planning—this vital work can't be delegated to advisors. His book shows wealthy families how to spot "flashpoints" of potential discord, how to organize themselves around their wealth, how to form family councils, and how to develop self-mediation skills to deal with family differences that inevitably arise. Drawing on the new positive psychology, the Le Van offers fresh and encouraging insights into family happiness, and how happiness can be attained and maintained by wealthy families.

Gerald Le Van is a trust and estates lawyer and former law professor with more than twenty years' experience mediating family disputes about money and business. "Healthy Wealth in Families" is his sixth book. His other books include:

The Survival Guide for Business Families (Routledge 1998)
Raising Rich Kids (Xlibris 2003)
Families Money and Trouble (Xlibris 2003)
Lawyers Lives Out of Control (WorldCom Press 1992)

Foreword

Like it or not, wealthy families are joined at the wallet.

- Healthy wealthy families handle their interdependent wallet elegantly. They proudly fly a green flag signifying family peace and mutual enjoyment.

- In divided families, joint wealth fuels feuds that can incinerate precious irreplaceable relationships. Theirs is a red flag of combat.

- Too many families cower under a yellow flag of apprehension and indecision. Their common wallet is a mixed bag. Fearing that shared wealth might divide them, they maintain uneasy, unhealthy, unpleasant distances. Lack of communication eventually ignites discord.

I mediate family disputes about money and business. Our client families are joined at the wallet. For more than twenty years, I have observed the impact of shared wealth on family relationships. Irate family members may insist, "This dispute is not about money!" … But it is. It's always about money or else I wouldn't be called in.

But it's always about *more* than money. It's not the money … altogether. Then what is it, other than money, that so riles blood kin? Why *sue* each other over money, thereby putting at risk those precious irreplaceable relationships built up over generations of patient nurturing?

We have interviewed thousands of wealthy relatives. We have moderated their discussions, mediated their discord, managed and monitored their reconciliations. We have been extraordinarily successful at keeping wealthy families out of the courthouse—or at least we've been on the scene when they settled things.

In the course of our mediating experience, some guideposts and warning signs have emerged. A guidepost: it's seldom productive to discuss how a wealthy relative spends his or her money. One risks sounding critical and starting an argument. A warning sign: it's clearly unhealthy for a wealthy family *not* to discuss their shared wealth, or worse, to treat money as a taboo.

This is not a comprehensive discussion of family wealth. Rather, I point out seventy guideposts and warning signs to families searching for healthier wealth. Most importantly, I focus on the *relational estate*—a wealthy family's most valuable non-financial asset. In yellow- or red flag families, their relational estate is both the source of discord and the arena where that discord can be managed and resolved. For most families, their relational estate is priceless.

Black Mountain, North Carolina
May 2007

Part One

"It's Not the Money ...
Altogether!"

Some Guideposts and Warning Signs:

1. A family's *relational estate* is that complex mix of genes, history, heritage, and web of intimate relationships that connects them across generations. It is their most valuable non-financial asset. It is priceless.

2. Families aren't just random clusters of individuals who happen to be genetically related. Families are intricate systems that struggle to provide us stability, constancy, tradition, heritage, acceptance—a sense of belonging.

3. Most kids begin to develop lifetime attitudes about money between ages eleven and fourteen.

4. Connecting with another's story is at the heart of human communication.

5. A father's unburdening cannot be postponed until his son is old enough to understand. The time is never right for both of them. The very difference in their ages forces the exchange before either is ready—or else sustains a barrier of silence.

6. A continual parenting dilemma is when, where or whether to hang on, to let go, or to seek a healthy in-between I call "letting grow".

7. The antipathy generated by a family lawsuit will be transmitted down to younger generation family members in ways older family members cannot anticipate, cannot trace, and cannot control. Family lawsuits rip and tear

relational estates that have taken generations to build, then hand the shreds to future generations.

1

Your Family's Most Valuable Non-financial Asset: Your "Relational Estate"

I mediate family disputes about money.

The family dispute is always about money, but it's also always about more than money. It's not the money … altogether. It's also about the *relational estate*—the family's most precious non-financial asset.

For years I've been searching for a way to describe what's most valuable to a wealthy family, other than its financial wealth. Some suggest we call that non-financial something the "relational estate" and I like the words. "Relational estate" was first coined by divorce lawyers to describe the remnant relationship between ex-spouses that survives their divorce. Their remnant relational estate affects children and extended family, a web of shared friendships, and their participation in such post-divorce events as graduations, marriages, births and funerals.

Consider the relational estate of any family, wealthy or not, healthy or not. It includes genes, history and heritage. It encompasses the whole web of interpersonal relationships that connects them across generations. Their relational estate continues to include even deceased family members. In the words of lyricist Stephen Sondheim, "they die, but they don't".

Though intangible and impossible to quantify, your family's relational estate is enormously valuable to those who share it. Don't overlook its critical importance.

Family disputes about money or business aren't really resolved unless change takes place in the relational estate.

2

Families and Porcupines: A Primer on Family Systems

To understand a family's relational estate, view the family as a system. Here's a quick introduction to family systems.

At wedding rehearsal dinners, my wife toasts the bride and groom:

> "May your marriage be like two porcupines snuggling down on a cold night: close enough for warmth, but not so close that you prick each other."

Some guests titter, then an ex-roommate tells a long embarrassing story about the bride's or groom's ex-squeeze, and the porcupines are forgotten.

Asked why his teams mostly ran the football, legendary Texas coach Darrell Royal replied, "Three things can happen to a forward pass, and two of them are bad." Imagine an extended family of porcupines—six, eleven, fourteen—all snuggled down on a cold night. Three things can happen to a porcupine in a nest of other porcupines, and two of them are bad. Too close to other porcupines and you get pricked; too distant and it's too chilly. The trick is to stay close enough for maximum warmth and minimum pricking.

Nested porcupines can't just lie there in one position. Suppose another porcupine rolls over or stretches. One leaves for another nest. Another brings back a mate. Little porcupines are born. Two big ones fight. An old porcupine sickens or dies. To maximize warmth and minimize pricking, you must constantly change your position relative to other porcupines.

Your family, my family, we are like those porcupines in the nest, forever shifting and changing to maximize warmth and minimize pricking. We're a system, a family system. That's the way psychologists view families and I think they're on to something.

If there is a problem, it's not just the one or two family members directly involved. Those problems reverberate throughout the family system. Everyone is affected. All change positions in response to the problem.

Those of us who work with families professionally look first at the family system. How did things get that way, and how would a change reverberate throughout the system? Suppose a family hero is tarnished, or the family black sheep reforms. The system needed a hero to galvanize family pride. It also needed a black sheep as a lightning rod for family anxieties. Families systems can be very static, very slow to change. Contrary to the facts sometimes, the family may continue to revere the tarnished hero or continue to dump on the reformed black sheep. Why? Because the system "worked" that way.

Families aren't just random clusters of individuals who happen to be genetically related. Families are intricate systems that struggle to provide us stability, constancy, tradition, heritage, acceptance—a sense of belonging.

Our families remind us continually of where we came from and who we are. Family systems may grow fast yet change slowly. A few are crazy or cold or uncaring. Most manage to make a place for us—with maximum warmth and minimum pricking.

Psychotherapists use "family system" to describe the emotional dynamics at work inside the relational estate. My porcupine image underscores how emotional events reverberate throughout the entire system.

Your family's relational estate is the vessel that gathers and transmits genes, history (including these emotional events), heritage and relationships across the generations.

Pass it down with great care.

It's not the money … altogether.

3

Joined at the Wallet: Like it or Not

I define a "business family" as two or more relatives who own valuable property together. Business and family are entwined, overlap, are difficult if not impossible to separate.

A business family may be partners in a family partnership. They may be beneficiaries of an estate or trust. They may be common owners of a stock portfolio, a shopping center, or an art collection. A business family may own an active operating company—a "family business". Whether close or distant, affectionate or cold, by definition a business family is nevertheless a family system joined at the wallet.

Some business families handle their interdependent finances elegantly. Somehow the common wallet binds them closer together. Together they savor their shared good fortune. They enjoy each others' enjoyment. They are generous with each other. They may disapprove of how some relatives spend their money, but they don't say so. They talk with each other freely and frankly about the family money, finding ways to differ without being disagreeable.

In other business families, the common wallet is feud fuel that eventually incinerates precious parts of their family relationship. Contemporary Hatfields and McCoys hurl insults and hire lawyers to terrorize each other. Old slights and injustices become magnified, quantified, monetized. Their primal needs for each other, their primal instincts of loyalty to family, their connection to a common history—all are casualties in the war to win a fatter portion of the common wallet.

In too many business families, joinder at the wallet both binds and loosens. For fear that money differences might divide them, they maintain a mutual distance, lest intimacy ignite. Their opinions about investment or family management have an edge if expressed, or smolder if suppressed. Disapproving comments about how others spend their family money—or live on it instead of work-ing—slip out at inappropriate times. For fear that frank discussions of money could impair more precious parts of the family relationship, they don't talk about it.

Joinder at the wallet is neither good nor bad. But it isn't neutral either. Joinder at the wallet usually binds or divides.

If your business family pretends a non-existent consensus, or denies or buries your differences, you may be caught up in wallet waffling and that could degener-ate to wallet war. Talk together about your concerns. Give joinder at the wallet a chance to bind you closer together.

It's not the money ... altogether, of course. But how we handle our joint family wallet is a powerful force—for good or ill—in the vessel of our relational estate that we're passing down to our children and grandchildren.

4

Sex, Money and Kids: Don't Create a Taboo

When our older daughter was about nine, she bounced up on the bed beside me with a question:

"Why do I look like you, Daddy?

"Mama told me to ask you."

Having two younger siblings, Mama's role in shaping her nine-year old body was obvious. My role was not.

Recently, I asked my daughter, now a mother herself, if she remembered asking that question. She didn't. Nor do I remember how I answered. Her adolescent daughters overheard us and giggled.

I like a three-step approach to children's hard questions:

First, affirm the child's curiosity. "That's a neat question. I'm glad you look like me!" Be careful about creating a taboo, "That's a naughty question!", or ridiculing, "That's a silly thing to ask!", or putting them off, "You'll understand when you're older." If we don't attempt an answer now, they'll probably suspect there's something sinister, or else we don't trust them with the information.

Second, answer truthfully. Forget about the stork. If you aren't sure, do some homework. "Let me think about that until tomorrow."

Third, answer within the child's current ability to understand. A nine-year old doesn't need to know everything just yet.

Though most modern families can talk about sex, money seems to be the last taboo for family discussion. Suppose my nine-year-old daughter had asked,

"Daddy, are we *rich?*"

I would reach again for the same three-step approach.

First, affirm curiosity, "That's a neat question—everyone's curious about money."

Second, a truthful answer. Here's a chance to recount our blessings.

> "Most people in the world don't have what we have or live like we live. We have a house, a car, a TV, good food, good schools and good health care. We are free as anyone, and safe as anyone from dangers and dictators. Lots of third world people would say we're rich. Lots of third world people live on less than two dollars a day."

> "But Daddy, are we rich *Americans?*"

A character in my book "Raising Rich Kids" says you're a rich American if you can maintain a high lifestyle indefinitely, without working, and with minimal risk of losing what you have. Most nine-year-olds can understand that. A truthful answer needn't go into the numbers.

Of course there's the risk of over-explaining. Our son once asked his Mama a question. Trying to be helpful, she replied "Why don't you ask Daddy?" She got a thoughtful response,

> "Because, Mama, I don't want to know that much about it."

Most kids begin to develop lifetime attitudes about money between ages eleven and fourteen. If parents don't talk with them about money, they'll take their cues from peers, television and movies, the Internet, and from their early adolescent perceptions of their parents' behavior.

Don't make money a family taboo.

Your relational estate transmits taboos.

5

Feuds and Flashpoints: Unloading Family Buckshot

When my grandfather's younger brother, John Calhoun Bell, was county attorney in western Colorado, the local doctor challenged him to a duel. It seems that Uncle John had disapproved some of the doc's charges to the county for treating the poor. The doctor had interpreted this as an assault on his honor as a gentleman. It was 1876. Friends assured Uncle John it was a bluff, so he accepted the challenge. But the sawbones wasn't bluffing. The code of the West called for double-barreled shotguns at twenty yards.

Like other men in my mother's family, Uncle John was gentle and thoughtful and witty, a most unlikely duelist. Nevertheless, with great fear and trembling, he showed up at Dead Man's Gulch on the appointed Sunday morning. Lawyer and doctor paced off the ten yards in opposite directions, then turned and fired. Neither fell. Their seconds had emptied all the buckshot from the shells. Uncle John lived on into his eighties, became a judge and served five terms in Congress.

That aggrieved doctor should have sued Uncle John. Dueling was against the law on the Colorado frontier, as it is everywhere today. Civility, it is said, has moved our grievances from Dead Man's Gulch to the courtroom. Yet recently, a judge who lost patience with opposing lawyers locked in a nasty personal battle before him growled, "This case makes me lament the demise of dueling, but I cannot order a duel and thus reduce the number of counsel I have to put up with!"

Duels between families we call feuds. The Hatfields and the McCoys had intermarried. Except for the shotguns, some courtroom feuds between family members are reminiscent of Dead Man's Gulch. I can understand an impatient judge who would like to order an old-fashioned feud, if he could.

11

My job is to prevent courtroom feuds between family members over money. What is it, other than the money, that's worth ripping and tearing precious family relationships built by generations of patient nurture? I call that "something other" a "flashpoint".

Flashpoints start arguments about money, generate conflicts, provoke lawsuits. Like lightning, some flashpoints are beyond our control. Someone in the older generation, now dead, shortchanged a sister, whose children want to square things. How do they right the wrong without unhinging the family?

Like embers, some flashpoints will burn away and cause no harm. Someone in the older generation, now dead, shortchanged a sister, who has forgiven, or forgotten, or let it pass. Her children decide not to go there.

Like glowing coals in an unattended campfire, some flashpoints smolder, waiting for the wind to blow them into the woods. Flashpoints smolder in people—who are dissatisfied, feel undervalued, left out, unappreciated, disappointed, misunderstood. Flashpoints smolder in relationships—rivalries, jealousies, estrangements, between relatives who don't speak. Flashpoints smolder in circumstances—poor health, accidents, misfortune, tragedy.

All too often, it's lawyers' wind that blows smoldering flashpoints into the woods. So don't leave family campfires unattended. Empty the buckshot if you can.

My job as mediator is to unload the buckshot.

Don't pass down smoldering flashpoints in your relational estate.

Do your best to douse the campfire, or at least spread the coals before a troubling wind blows them into the woods.

6

Thanks, Colombo: Asking the Right Questions the Right Way

Do you remember Colombo ... that rumpled TV rerun detective in the wrinkled raincoat, played by Peter Faulk?

Colombo painstakingly pieces people's stories together to solve crimes. Wise Colombo knows he can't discover what's really going on inside another person—guilt or innocence, what she may think or feel, or what motivates her. He can try to connect with her story, and that connection may tell him what he needs to know. Connecting with another's story is at the heart of human communication. A wise Colombo keeps asking "Please help me understand your story".

Colombo lets her know he's struggling to understand. He doesn't intimidate, or cross-examine. If there are gaps or inconsistencies, he doesn't attack the storyteller. Instead of: "What do you mean by ...," Colombo faults his own understanding. "I'm having trouble with ..." Clever yet fumbling, he blames himself. "Please be patient with a dumb cop."

Colombo listens to the whole story, all of it. He doesn't pick and choose what he wants to hear—like TV detective Sgt. Joe Friday of Dragnet, "Just the facts Ma'm". If the storyteller wanders off point, Colombo reassures: "Go ahead Ma'm ... I got time."

The witness' storyline may be complex, twisted, even perverse, but it's her plot. The plot has meaning to the storyteller, and her meaning is important. Her story may mean something different to him, but he doesn't say. "What do you make of all this, Ma'm?"

13

Colombo doesn't ask a question if there's a better way to get the information he needs. Mostly, he questions his own understanding. Once begun, the Q&A pattern is hard to break. Q&A would teach the witness that it's up to Colombo to ask questions, and it's up to her to answer. Q&A would tell her that Colombo's the boss, that only Colombo knows what's important or relevant, so she doesn't volunteer. Except to answer, she would keep her mind and heart closed. Colombo's especially careful with "why" questions because they connote disapproval, displeasure, and insinuate that the witness has done wrong or behaved badly. "Why" questions put her on the defensive.

Colombo watches non-verbal communications, body language, what people tell him without trying. He's alert to tenseness, rigid posture, clenched hands, facial expressions, dress, physical condition, gait, tears. If tears come, or the witness rages, Colombo's sympathetic: "Gosh Ma'm, I'm sorry you're upset", never "Let's not get emotional!" Colombo knows that each of us is 100% correct about the way we *feel*. Colombo listens for feelings: "Please help me hear the music, Ma'm."

Colombo listens carefully for the first and last words spoken. Her opening sentence may tell him what's uppermost on her mind. Her closing sentence may express how she perceives their relationship: trust or suspicion, affection or disgust.

If she shifts the conversation abruptly, it may be a defensive maneuver, away from something she doesn't want to discuss. Clever Colombo counters, "Did you want to say more about …?" Colombo listens for recurrent themes and references that reveal deep unspoken concerns. "I believe you mentioned … several times. Is there something more you wanted me to know about that?"

Colombo tries not to describe the witness' behavior, only his own reactions to it. Colombo will say, "I sense you were distracted", rather than, "You weren't paying attention". Then he follows with something like, "Would it help if we went over that again?"

Colombo may want to tell the witness how she's coming across, but he prefers to be invited. He waits for her to say something like, "Do you think I'm being selfish?" or "Does it sound as though I'm fooling myself about this matter?" If she doesn't invite feedback, Colombo invites himself, "Would you like to know what I'm hearing so far?"

Colombo's wily understanding of human communication applies far beyond law enforcement. We can't know what's going on inside others, but we can try to understand their stories. In close relationships, we share stories, ours and theirs. In families, we're the story we tell each other without speaking. But it helps to tell and retell it.

"We don't communicate very well", confess most of my client families. So often, a big part of my job is to help unscrew skewed communications. Thanks, Colombo.

Habits of comfortable communication are invaluable self-mediating skills if family discord arises.

7

Fathers and Sons: Their Unresolved Issues

In the classic movie, "East of Eden", James Dean painfully portrayed an agonized son who cannot gain his father's approval. This theme recurs in the recent movie "Luther". The young priest Martin Luther is tortured by a perceived inability to please either his earthly father or his heavenly father.

Too often, I witness the replay of this same sad theme. But not always. I do see many healthy and wholesome relationships between fathers and sons.

I have tried to portray a classic father-son dilemma in a scene from my novel, "Families Money and Trouble". Jay JacMar and his thirty-year old son, Tripp, are traveling together on a long international flight. Tripp just has goaded his father into a soul-baring conversation, and now regrets it.

> Ordinarily controlled, polite, taciturn, shy, introverted, enigmatic, Jay had begun to unpack his soul. Tripp felt embarrassed and uncomfortable, as though his father were standing naked before him.

> Tripp felt unworthy to share these intimate confidences. He was too young to resonate, too immature to empathize with the accumulated frustrations and late life ambitions of this very complicated man—confidences Jay could better share with his closest friend.

> A father's unburdening cannot be postponed until his son is old enough to understand. The time is never right for both of them. The very difference in their ages forces the exchange before either is ready—or else sustains a barrier of silence. Nor can it occur without the spoken words, however halting or ill-chosen. No silent understanding can spark the gap between father and son.

Except to shake hands, Tripp hadn't touched his father in years. Tripp shifted his position, put his shoulder against his father's, and dozed. Feeling his son against him Jay dozed also.

Jay had announced his retirement as CEO of the family business. Tripp hints strongly that he plans to succeed Jay as president of the company, but so far Jay hasn't taken the hint. Earlier in their conversation, Jay talked about his own father, Jack, the company's founder:

> "When Jack was alive I really wanted to run this company. Thought I had earned it. Thought I deserved it. Then suddenly Jack was dead and I had the job. I was terrified.

> "Jack ran the whole show. Everyone reported to him.

> "Sometimes he acted like the company was his favorite child and his sons were annoyances. He took our suggestions as personal criticism, fought us when we tried to improve things. Once he called my MBA degree a 'nuisance'.

> "Now and then he intimated we were paid more than we were 'worth'. That's hard to take from your father."

Tripp began as a successful investment banker on Wall Street, but returned home to the family business "to claim his heritage." Jay concluded that Tripp wasn't yet ready to lead the company. Remembering his painful inability to please his own father, how was Jay to defer Tripp's premature request?

> The JacMars worked together in that atmosphere of nodding grunting uncommunication so common in business families. They clung to unuttered understandings cluttered with murky misunderstandings.

Family businesses are replete with tensions between father-leaders who continue to hang on, and sons who are impatient for them to step aside. His father's approval, or disapproval, is a deeply powerful emotional force in a son's life. From his own experience, Jay understood that saying "no" to his son about succession could be taken as disapproval.

Fathers who must say "not yet" need also explain how their sons can further prepare themselves for eventual leadership. This was Jay JacMar's dilemma. Fathers who must say, "no, never" must affirm and express in words their continuing love, acceptance and support of deeply disappointed sons. And this can be very, very hard. The time is never right for either of them.

8

Lance Armstrong's Training Wheels: "Letting Grow"

Some thirty years ago, an anxious parent removed the training wheels from Lance Armstrong's tiny two-wheeler. No doubt Lance wobbled, fell a few times, skinned a knee or an elbow. When Lance left the sidewalk to ride in the street, their anxiety increased.

A continual parenting dilemma is when, where or whether to hang on, to let go, or to seek a healthy in-between I call "letting grow". As children grow older, more independent, and the risks of their bad judgment increase, parents' search for "letting grow" becomes more complicated.

Picture Lance Armstrong, riding a state-of-the-art racing bike in the Tour de France, but with training wheels still attached. That's how some frustrated adult beneficiaries in wealthy families view themselves. The training wheels are still attached to their finances. They long to balance on two wheels and ride in the street with their financially self-parenting peers.

For some beneficiaries there is no choice. The financial training wheels are welded to frame by rigid legal documents. For others, the training wheels are bolted to the frame, removable at the discretion of trustees.

Every day, those in business make a fundamental choice: operate, sell, or liqui-date the company. Trustees with the discretion to distribute make similar choices: hang on, let go, or "let grow". Hang on, withhold distributions, and avoid improvident expenditures by beneficiaries. Or let go, pay it out, and hope that it isn't spent foolishly.

A very wise "let grow" professional trustee I know holds a budget conference with adult beneficiaries at the beginning of each year. Her approach over discretionary distributions is quite simple: "Please keep me from ever having to say 'No'". So long as budgeting works, the beneficiaries don't seem bothered by the training wheels.

"Letting grow" may mean including beneficiaries in investment reviews, investment decision-making, or naming them as co-trustees. Eventually, "letting grow" may mean no review at all of what beneficiaries do with their distributions.

Whatever course it takes, "letting grow" is wisely proactive about removing the training wheels.

Go Lance!

9

Divided Families:
Civil Disengagement Instead of
War

"A house divided against itself cannot stand" warned Abraham Lincoln, quoting Aesop and the Bible. Lincoln concluded that war was inevitable in order to preserve the Union. Is there an alternative to war in a divided family?

The law assumes that all human relationships will ultimately fail, whereupon every individual will need a lawyer to protect him or her from everyone else … even from family. The law assumes that family war over money is inevitable.

But a family house divided cannot withstand litigation. No matter how carefully their lawyers try to prepare them for battle, families have no idea—and cannot possibly foresee—how dreadful a family lawsuit can become.

Litigation divides families into opposing camps. Until it's resolved they may quit talking and communicate solely through lawyers. The antipathy generated by a family lawsuit will be transmitted down to younger family members in ways older family members cannot anticipate, cannot trace, and cannot control.

Certain aspects of family are not divisible. Genes, history, and heritage—in some form—will survive legal hostilities. But why burden inheritance with the lethal fallout from family litigation? A family bitterly divided today, may yet yen to reunite in a later generation. Even the blood feuding Hatfields and the McCoys eventually buried the hatchet.

The opposite extremes: either a family war or else complete family reconciliation now, are not the only alternatives. If family enmity runs too deep to resolve currently, "civil disengagement" may be a viable alternative.

Civil disengagement:

- acknowledges currently irreconcilable differences,

- but avoids family litigation;

- manages each divided camp separately,

- but leaves the door open to family reunification in later generations.

"We can't get along now, but who knows, perhaps our grandchildren may enjoy each other." Civil disengagement can leave them that unfettered legacy.

Armies are composed of divisions. Lots of successful companies operate through divisions. In the interest of present peace and the welfare of future generations, a divided family can civilly disengage into separate divisions for a generation ... or two.

And who knows?

Once civilly disengaged, those divided houses may miss each other.

10

Litigation: The Family "Doomsday Machine"

At the climax of the cult movie "Dr. Strangelove", the Soviet Union unleashes its "Doomsday Machine", a destructive device so powerful that once activated, it can't be shut down. In many ways a family lawsuit resembles the "Doomsday Machine." Its destructive power can't be recalled. Everyone loses. Nobody wins.

Fulton Oursler wrote many books, including "The Greatest Story Ever Told", a popular account of Jesus' life, later made into a movie. Under an assumed name, Oursler's second wife, Grace wrote rather torrid (for the times) love stories. Fulton and Grace had two children; Fulton also had two other children by a prior marriage. Fulton's will left everything to Grace. When Grace later died, her will left everything to their two younger children, but nothing at all to Fulton's two older children. The omitted older children claimed that Grace had promised Fulton to leave them equal shares, and brought a lawsuit to enforce their claim.

The outcome of the lawsuit is unimportant at this point. But its effect on the family presents a sober lesson. In his memoirs, Will Oursler, one of the older children, describes its effects. Here are some excerpts.

> It was a battle I did not seek, did not want—brother and sister against brother and sister, love against love, hate against hate. I did not seek it, but I had no escape. The challenge was there. And if I did not wish to battle for myself, I still could not leave Helen (the other child of the first marriage) and her children to go the road alone.

> To accept passively would be to believe that my father did not love my sister Helen and me, that he loved only the children of his second marriage, April

and Tony. It would be to believe that my father wanted two of his children to live in luxury on the money he had earned, and the other two to know nothing but the earnings they struggled for ...

It is an experience to be disinherited. Of a sudden there is a brand upon you, the letter etched into your flesh. You should feel guilty. But guilty for what? Of being born? For if you had not been born, Grace would have faced no problems, no lonely set of children to remind her of another wife.

You turn to lawyers and courts to seek a remedy, if remedy there be. Could I go to them and ask them to give us money their mother left to them?

In the hands of the law, lawyers, legalism, of procedures, delays, and tactics, you are no longer yourself or even your own master. Abruptly, you are part of this too, and your lawyer informs you that introducing testimony about some of the facts might be painful. But this is the way of the law and courts; this is the meaning of conflict between human beings, the bitterness of conflict.

We made our claim for a share of our father's estate. It went on for five years, the battle that hung above our lives like a smoky cloud. Helen and I were asking only for the shares that would have come to us, and for our children the share that would have come to them, under the terms of Grace's original will ...

While the battle of brother and sister against brother and sister went on in the courts, so also it went on in our lives, with no word between these two sets of children beyond the legalisms of complaints and answers and pretrial interrogations ...

All this time the case went on, the battle of briefs and counter-briefs. There was an effort at settlement, and April and Tony and Helen and I had several meetings, through which would occasionally glow the feeling that we were truly brothers and sisters.

For a few weeks it almost seemed as though a settlement were possible; it almost seemed as though the flickering flame of brotherhood was coming alive. But it, too, died in the suffocating questions that arose—lawyers' bills and which side was to pay them, questions of who was right and wrong at this time or that. The lawyers tried to work it out and failed; we all tried to work it out and failed. The staggering legal fees remained to be met, and unanswered questions that dogged us remained.

Grimly, like a Greek tragedy, the plot went on and we returned to court. For this breakdown in negotiations that could have made us all more content I don't blame April and Tony. I blame the four of us—and Grace and Fulton, the past, all our lives.

There were too many problems, too much involvement with lawyers and fees and bills to be paid. And below the surface perhaps the chasm had become too great to bridge.

We were bothers and sisters, but we could not agree. Once more the case went back to the courts ... April and Tony won, four to three and it was over.

There are no villains in this family story. What can I be but sorry for what Grace has done to Helen and to me, to April and to Tony, to Fulton's grandchildren, most of all for what she did to herself? Can I find it in my heart to hold rancor, where there is only pity and sorrow for the woman of many gifts and accomplishments who suffered bitter insecurity and guilt? She was bewildered and confused, torn by conflict. And her last gesture, incomprehensible to Helen and me, left our family irreparably estranged.

11

A Family Lawsuit:
Advance Damage Control

In my novel, "Families Money and Trouble", a family lawsuit appears inevitable. Disgruntled family members have circulated an advance copy of a complaint against the top officers of JacMar Corporation, the family company. Named defendants are Jay JacMar, the founder's son and CEO, and his is his sister, Karen, the company CFO. The complaint alleges that both have wrongfully abused their executive positions.

The mediator is speaking to Jay and Karen:

"Family lawsuits get out of hand in a hurry.

"If the JacMars are going to court you need to contain the damage. You need to draw some family boundaries that litigation can't cross. Otherwise, family litigation is a wild animal on a rampage. It will poison everything and every-one in sight.

"So I have some homework for you. I want you to make some lists.

"First, list some family blessings about JacMar Corporation, who should be thanked for what and why.

"Second, list what you do and don't want to happen during the lawsuit and why.

"Finally, list what should be done with your lists—who should see them and under what circumstances.

In response, Karen JacMar drafts the following:

Karen's Manifesto

1. Jack and Margaret JacMar have left us with abundant opportunities and lifestyles we have not earned.

2. We are the beneficiaries:

   - of Jack's energy, ambition and hard work,
   - of Margaret's love, nurture and vigor,
   - of Jay's vision, intellect and quiet leadership,
   - of Frank's warmth, wit and charm,
   - of Frances' courage, strength and compassion, and the dedication of [her sons] Frank Jr. and Ernest to our Company, and
   - of Karen's versatility, loyalty and team play.

3. JacMar Corporation is an important part of our family heritage. The Company has provided us with careers, prominence and personal wealth.

4. Yet we differ on important issues involving Company management. We hope our differences will be settled through negotiation or mediation. If not, they will be resolved by court decision.

5. Our differences are straining our relationships with each other and we anticipate further stress. We urgently desire to avoid unnecessary injury to our connectedness.

6. Our remedies are limited to money damages. None of us subverts the importance of family to money demands. None of us will use litigation as an arena to expose rivalries, envies, injustices, hurts, slights or neglects.

7. We wish to minimize publicity, sensationalism and erroneous reporting. None of us will communicate with the media about our differences or the litigation. We will instruct our lawyers to refrain from any public comment about our case. We will seek to have all records of this matter sealed from public inspection.

8. A continuing healthy family relationship is our highest priority. We want to remain a strong family after this matter is concluded, regardless of its outcome.

9. We are particularly concerned that our differences may adversely affect relationships between our children and grandchildren. We will do all we can to confine our disputes to our own generation.

10. We urge our respective attorneys to be respectful and courteous to all family members at all stages of this matter. We ask them not to expose or exploit past disputes or differences between us that are not directly related to management of the Company. We ask all judges, magistrates and mediators to cooperate in our objective to protect our family relationship.

Karen sends an email to the mediator attaching her draft "manifesto". It reads:

What do you think of sending the attached to the other side?

Ask for their comments and suggestions?

If they don't buy in, OK. We can abide by it unilaterally can't we?

Maybe this will look better to them as the litigation progresses.

Maybe it would interest the judge or jury.

I guess the family could reconsider this even after final judgment.

Karen

Family lawsuits threaten to shatter the precious vessel that contains the relational estate.

All such lawsuits do great damage, leaving future generations to piece together whatever shards remain.

Karen proposes damage control.

Part Two

When the Family is in Business

Some Guideposts and Warning Signs:

8. For families in business together, work and family overlap at every turn, love and work are inextricably intertwined. As of old, the family is the common source of both.

9. The good news is that strong business families are the strongest competitors in the market place.

10. A non-family company cannot acquire, synthesize or fake the unique family virtues.

11. Their relational estate can be a huge off-balance sheet asset for family companies—or a huge off-balance sheet liability.

12. Dialogue accesses knowledge that is otherwise inaccessible to individuals inquiring alone.

13. Silence is terribly ambiguous—and threatening. Silence can mean anything. When another is silent we assume the worst.

14. American individualism may have won the West, but twenty-first century Americans live most of our lives in relationships—in those passageways that connect us with other people.

15. Communication connects us. Misunderstanding divides us. Loners can't know what they could discover by dialogue.

16. One earns sweat equity. One is born to blood equity. The root cause of most conflict about family compensation is failure to honor the difference.

17. Compensation for work done has three major components, each rewarding different incentives: basic salary or wages is payment for trying; a bonus is for excelling; retirement benefits reward longevity and loyalty.

18. Either way—step down or sell—sounds like the business leader's death itself. Is it better to falter as an aging autocrat than endure the slow suicide of succession?

19. The business leader need not be abandoned, ignored, or cast aside. The aging business leader can play a vital role on his children's new management team as invited coach and teacher.

20. Sooner or later, inactive shareholders will cause trouble.

21. Parents who assume the company must be divided equally among the children, may learn the children don't want it that way.

22. Regardless of how well the family gets along now, don't count on harmony forever.

23. Mid-life crisis is like waking up on a small boat in a storm. Change jobs, and the storm follows you. Seek escape by working longer and harder, have more children, and the storm intensifies.

24. It's challenging to choose new leaders from inside your organization. It's more difficult to choose them from inside your family. Either way, you're too close to be objective.

12

Love and Work: Quiet Good News about Family Business

A newspaper reporter once asked Sigmund Freud to identify the sources of self-esteem and meaning in life. "Love and work" answered Dr. Freud, the founder of modern psychology.

For some, their family is the source of both love and work. Until two hundred years ago that's the way it was for most families. Families worked together on farms. Then during the 18th century our sources of love and work began to separate. Families migrated from farms to cities. Fathers worked in factories or shops away from their wives and children. By the end of the 20th century the majority of American mothers worked outside the home.

For most of us today, our source of work is detached from our source of love. Work issues and family issues overlap only as they compete for our time, attention, energies and loyalties. Some of us change jobs if work threatens family well-being. Others subordinate family to career. Most juggle.

For families in business together, work and family overlap at every turn, love and work are inextricably intertwined. As of old, the family is the common source of both.

Attention to business families intensified in the 1980s as legions of WWII veteran entrepreneurs approached retirement age. They hadn't set out to create a family business. It just happened as their families grew. Thousands of their children had been enticed into the family company with generous pay and perks underscored with tantalizing promises like "some day this will all be yours."

Passing the torch proved unexpectedly difficult. Founders resisted appeals to step aside, brothers and sisters jockeyed to succeed their fathers. Spouses and in-laws joined the fray. Meanwhile the business media spread noisy bad news about family fights and family lawsuits, mostly ignoring the quiet good news about most business families who learned to manage their differences and move on.

The good news is that strong business families are the strongest competitors in the market place. They are bound together by trust, love and loyalty. If the family sells the company to an outsider, those valuable assets disappear. A non-family company cannot acquire, synthesize or fake those basic family virtues.

As a long time consultant and mediator to business families, I witness both the good news and the bad. In families where the news is not good, suspicion challenges trust, love is strained by rivalries, family loyalty is subordinated to personal ambition. My job is to help turn families away from the bad news and to discover the good news about themselves.

Indeed, some business families must turn to outsiders to turn them away from the bad news they've created. Others could turn themselves around with some encouragement and direction.

For more than half the U.S. gross domestic product is generated by family businesses.

The quiet good news is that love and work in many family businesses is working!

13

The "Soft Side" of Business: Clocks and Rain Forests

There's lots of buzz about the "hard side" and the "soft side" in business today.

For two centuries, "hard side" thinking has dominated business. Harnessing logic and data, physics and mathematics, hard side companies have generated a technological revolution.

The hard side world is a clock. Successful companies are machines, conceived by engineers and watched over by accountants to assure maximum productivity at minimum cost. If it can't be quantified, it isn't important. Workers are interchangeable parts in the organizational machine. "Human resources" suggests that workers are regarded as mere raw materials.

Companies on the cutting edge today challenge these hard side assumptions. From their perspective, the world is not as a clock but a rain forest. Business enterprises are not machines, but ecosystems whose survival depends on successful interactions with other ecosystems in a vast rain forest—the global economy.

Cutting edge companies are knowledge-based. Knowledge is carefully collected from and redistributed among employees, who, themselves, have become the company's most valuable assets—no longer mere raw material. How workers contribute to and utilize the company's valuable shared knowledge is an important measure of their job performance.

Cutting edge companies stress teamwork. Individual achievement has given way to working relationships; independence to interdependence; self-absorption and self-reliance to networking and connectedness. Indeed, the computer's ultimate contribution may not be quantification at all, but connectedness and communication through the Internet.

Hard side companies caution workers to leave their emotional lives outside the gate—except for fear and greed. Other emotions are suspect, "touchy-feely", weak, a sign of insufficient self-control. Feelings could clog the machine. As a result, hard side workers feel detached, isolated, and too often depressed.

Freud taught that love and work are our principal sources of meaning and self esteem. A classic study concludes that the most important source of employee morale is not so much the paycheck but a sense of accomplishment and recognition for that accomplishment. Cutting edge companies engage and leverage worker emotions on the job. Their emotional engines energize the system and generate gut loyalty to the company. Sam Walton understood this. Strong family-owned companies understand this better than most.

Strong family companies are the most formidable competitors in the marketplace. Core family assets of trust, love, and loyalty permeate the workplace.

Their relational estate can be a huge off-balance sheet asset for family companies—or a huge off-balance sheet liability.

That's why relational estate planning is so indispensable for family companies.

14

So Long, Loner:
It's Team Time

The next sentence may require heavy lifting, so give it a tug.

"Dialogue accesses knowledge that is otherwise inaccessible to individuals inquiring alone."

Whoa! Does that mean that when two or more people talk things over they learn stuff you can't find out all by yourself?

Yep, podnuh, that's it.

But what about the great American folk hero? The self-reliant pioneer? John Wayne?

Yep, so long, loner. It's team time.

Highly successful companies have learned that their most valuable assets don't appear on the books. These hidden assets are very important conversations between creative people whose dialogue accesses very valuable company knowledge.

There may be huge undisclosed liabilities also. Important conversations that should take place … but don't. Valuable knowledge isn't accessed if people aren't talking.

Conversation assets and hushed liabilities exist in most relationships—in multinational corporations, in business families, between spouses, between partners, between parents and children, between friends. Chances are, if we haven't talked, we haven't learned what we badly need to know.

Part of a mediator's job is to help people resolve differences that get out of hand. How often do I hear, "But we have an understanding!" only to discover that there is no such understanding. There's a misunderstanding because they haven't talked.

How often do I hear, "I teach by example", but without words the teacher takes a huge risk of being misunderstood. Silence is so terribly ambiguous—and threatening. Silence can mean anything. When another is silent we assume the worst.

Words can be ambiguous too, but at least words invite questions and questions invite clarification. The strong but silent type, alas John Wayne, risks being misunderstood. Deeds alone don't explain … can't explain.

American individualism may have won the West, but twenty first century Americans live most of our lives in relationships—in those passageways that connect us with other people. Our productive lives play out in those passageways.

Communication connects us. Misunderstanding divides us. Loners can't know what they could discover by dialogue. Here's that heavy lifting again: "Dialogue accesses knowledge otherwise inaccessible to those inquiring alone."

"But I'm not a good talker!" I know. We all struggle to find the right words to communicate really important things. That's why we need to explore, experiment, try, fail, then try again.

Stephen Covey is right on the mark when he advises, "Seek first to understand, then to be understood." The more important part of dialogue is listening—the laying on of ears.

15

Family Payrolls:
Sweat Equity and Blood Equity

Family payrolls range from sensible to downright whacky. Here's my take on compensation in business families.

"Sweat equity" entitles a relative to be paid for the useful work he or she contributes to the family enterprise. "Blood equity" entitles family members to distributions and benefits from the company solely because they are relatives.

One earns sweat equity. One is born to blood equity. The root cause of most conflict about family compensation is failure to honor the difference. Most compensation conflict involves unhealthy mixtures of the two.

A useful measure of sweat equity is the amount of compensation the company would have to pay a non-relative to do the same job held by a family employee. By this measure, some family members are under worked and overpaid, while others are overworked and underpaid.

To the extent a family employee is overpaid, his excess compensation reduces other relatives' blood equity. To the extent a family employee is underpaid, the cost savings increases other relatives' blood equity at his expense. The underpaid family employee is often comforted by vague assurances that, "Some day this will all be yours", implying that future ownership will eventually square things for low pay today. Equal pay for all family employees almost always generates sweat equity-blood equity imbalances: equal pay is seldom fair, and fair compensation is seldom equal.

Compensation for work done has three major components, each rewarding different incentives: basic salary or wages is payment for trying; a bonus is for excelling; retirement benefits reward longevity and loyalty. These three incentives can become lost in the family's eagerness to distribute company profits at minimum tax cost, or by family reluctance to pay relatives according to merit.

Whether they try hard or not, salaries and wages of family employees are usually generous. If unduly generous, overpayment can tie a family member to the company with golden handcuffs—he or she couldn't earn that much in the competitive job market.

Deserving unrelated employees may get bonuses, but the lion's share of the bonus pool usually goes to family employees, not for excelling, but more or less according to their share ownership. Blood equity trumps sweat equity.

Unless they're pretty outrageous, family salaries and bonuses are usually tax deductible to the family company. The outrageous portion could be taxed as a dividend, but dividend taxes are low now thanks to recent tax cuts.

Longtime unrelated employees may get retirement benefits, but family employees customarily get all the law allows, a vehicle to defer further distributions to family from company profits in tax efficient ways. Family loyalty and longevity aren't very relevant.

Lots of family payrolls reflect outdated tax strategies, or haven't been reviewed or updated, except for cost of living increases, since the most recent family employee was hired.

The best compensation structure is one that works for the family and the business. What works for one family would court disaster in another. Equal compensation for all avoids the delicate sweat equity question: "What are you *worth* to the family company?" Sometimes, however, worth to the company gets garbled with worth to the *family*, and that perception causes trouble. Be very careful and clear about your relatives' perceived worthiness.

Ordinarily, I favor a family compensation structure that recognizes and rewards differing sweat equity. But transitioning from an out of whack family payroll to a more sensible one, e.g. from equality to merit, can be an exceedingly delicate mid-course correction.

Happy landings.

16

The Aging Founder:
Back to the Jump Seat

Founders who sell their companies routinely agree to stay on as consultants to the new owners. Their consultant term averages three years, but most just wander off long before it expires. Their consultant role is rarely pleasant. They are rarely consulted. They watch helplessly while the new owners "don't keep up product quality and don't treat *my* people right." After selling his company for cash at a fabulous price, a founder client told me, "I feel like a general who has just surrendered."

"I'm turning the company over to my sons on January 1," said the founder of a highly successful company with deserved pride. "And what will you do on January 2?" I asked. After a long sigh he soberly replied, "I have no idea." Must he endure the same dismal letdown as the founder who sells to strangers? Not necessarily. Here are some suggestions for the entrepreneur who steps down—or rather, steps back.

Embrace your new partner, Mr. Age. That retiring founder must learn to partner with Mr. Age. Initially, that partnership seems dark and threatening. Mr. Age steals energy and memory, sows restlessness among his children, undermines his role as unquestioned autocrat. Mr. Age has replaced him with eager sons or daughters who don't yet understand the business, who cannot lead as well as he.

Mr. Age may inspire his children to sell their stock or even to sell the company the founder spent his lifetime building. Either way—step down or sell—sounds like the founder's death itself. Better to falter as an autocrat than endure the slow suicide of succession?

Sometime during the succession planning process, I ask the founder to list what important lessons his successors have already learned from him. Similarly, I ask the successors to list those important lessons they have learned from the founder. When they compare their respective lists with each other, the result is almost always upbeat. Then I ask the founder to list separately what the successors have left to learn from him, and the successors to list what he still needs to teach them. These meetings can be tense, but revealing in a positive way. Teaching and learning should flow in both directions. Founders may have much to learn from their successors.

In the past, I have described the succession process as similar to checking out a new pilot. First the founder sits in the captain's seat on the left, and the successor on the right in the first officer's seat. They fly all the routes together: operations, manufacturing, sales, finance, administration, important customers and vendors, important contacts. Then they switch seats until the successor can fly all the routes himself. Thereafter, the founder rides in the back cabin with the other passengers.

But that's not the way it is with many founders. After the successor is checked out, the founders don't sit in the back cabin. They continue the ride in a jump seat located just behind the pilots. From the jump seat they are available to pilots, but can't reach the controls or talk on the radio—only listen. Like check pilots on commercial or military aircraft, they watch the instruments, listen to radio traffic, observe other aircraft and answer pilots' questions and monitor pilots' performance.

Ambitious children can be a hand full. But at least they *care* about the company, and their caring needs the wise leverage only founders can provide. They need not be abandoned, ignored, or cast aside.

The founder can play a vital role on his children's new management team as invited coach and teacher. Mr. Age can help them understand that children who prefer to sell their gifted stock can nevertheless remain loyal to the family and remain grateful for the advantages the company has provided.

Wise founders leverage their new partnership with Mr. Age. They leverage the energies and memories of younger persons. They sow and cultivate among the young, the wisdom and perspective gained only over many years.

All from the jump seat.

17

Parasites vs. Plunderers: Tensions between Inside and Outside Shareholders

Whether Sallie Bingham was the heroine or the villainess in the most publicized family business melodrama of the 1980s, depends upon your point of view. Sallie's parents gave her the stock she later used as a weapon against them. The Bingham media empire was ultimately sold because Sally felt that her ideas—and her 4% interest in the companies—were not being accorded sufficient respect.

The Bingham experience is, unfortunately, too familiar in family business circles. When gifts of stock are made, future battle lines are drawn. On one side are the inactive shareholders, outsiders who regard the insiders as *plunderers* of their legacy. In the other camp are the insiders who view the outsiders as *parasites*.

Sooner or later inactive shareholders—"parasites" such as Sally Bingham—will cause trouble. They may view their shares as poor investments because they are too concentrated, offer too little return, and are subject to too much control by insiders who divulge too little information. Ordinarily, there is no market for parasites' shares except for other shareholders, who usually don't care to buy, at least not a "reasonable" price. Parasites contend that a "reasonable" price is what their shares would bring if the entire company were sold. They are unimpressed by discounts for minority lack of control or for lack of marketability.

Active shareholders (the "plunderers") see the outsiders, ("parasites") as detached investors, uninterested in the growth of the business, too interested in distributions, too vocal with advice and criticism, too willing to inject family concerns into business decisions. Some families work out these differences. But too few do it successfully.

In her book, "Passion and Prejudice", Sallie Bingham complains about the lack of communication in her family. She has a point. Too often the older generation does its estate planning in secret. There is no discussion with members of the younger generation, who may be asked to invest the rest of their lives in their inheritance—the family business. The younger generation learns the details only after an elder dies.

Estate planning without communication can be hazardous. *Intergenerational* estate planning works best where frank and free discussion takes place between the givers and the potential receivers.

One item the generations should discuss together is the inevitable parasite-plunderer scenario. Parents who assume the company must be divided equally among the children, may learn that the children don't want it that way. Sallie Bingham might have been perfectly satisfied with other assets, but no one asked her. They just gave her stock.

Regardless of how well the family gets along now, don't count on harmony forever. Old rivalries and jealousies, new in-laws, or something completely unforeseen can trigger a conflict between parasites and plunderers. Estate planning in the first generation is the very best time to head off the problem. This means *early* estate planning, before those annual gifts of voting shares begin. Even at $24,000, per year gift tax-free, those annual gifts of shares can add up over time. Sallie Bingham may have received her stock because her parents' advisors pushed for annual gifts that would escape tax. Annual gifts make estate planning sense, but annual gifts of voting shares in the family business *don't* make sense if they exacerbate the parasite-plunderer situation. If you can, give something else to the children who won't be working in the business.

If, like most family business owners, your assets are predominantly locked up in the company, one way you can create additional wealth is by investing in one of several breeds of life insurance. Life insurance for their joint lives could be purchased naming a child (or a trust for her) as owner and beneficiary. Part of the premium could be paid with $24,000 cash gifts to her each year.

Non-voting shares for inactive children may not be the answer. Depriving them of a *voice* in company affairs could rub salt in the wound. Shareholders who can't vote are at the mercy of those who can.

Unfortunately, most parents don't take this advice. They have already given equal shares of voting common stock to active and inactive children alike. What then?

Your outside board of directors can play an important role. Outside directors must represent *all* shareholders, active and inactive family members. Their job is to exercise their best judgment for the benefit of the company as a whole. Outside directors create a corporate culture of accountability. Their impartiality should regulate the flow of perquisites and dividends. Having outside board members is desirable for lots of good reasons. If the outside board keeps the lid on parasite-plunderer conflict, that alone is reason enough to justify its existence.

If shareholders balk at an outside board, at least try to expand communications among them. Circulate company financial information on a regular basis. Make annual shareholder meetings informative as well as cordial. Keep outsiders abreast of what is happening in the company. Call regular family meetings to discuss the business. Form a family council.

Perks alone won't work. If company hunting camps, aircraft, apartments and the like are available, make sure that all shareholders have fair access. Don't try to buy peace with your parasites by giving them perks such as cars, club memberships, and fringe benefits. Most times it just doesn't work. Perks-for-peace just gives them something else to argue about.

By all means, keep direct communications flowing. Discuss ways of buying out inactive shareholders, and keep that topic of conversation alive. Negotiate if you can. Get everyone to understand that sooner or later the parasite-plunderer tensions could destroy the business.

Keep your lawyer, accountant, and other advisors abreast of your discussions, but weigh carefully the consequences of asking your lawyer to speak for you to other family members. Smart families communicate directly with each other, not through third persons. Once families start communicating through lawyers, the risks of family war escalate dramatically. Of course, if there is serious talk of buying or selling, you will want your lawyer present for technical advice and negotiating skills.

18

Mid-Life Crisis in the Workplace: The Internal Storm

Not every thirtysomething or fortysomething experiences a mid-life crisis. But for those who do—men and women of all classes, races, and ethnicities—mid-life crisis is very real.

Mid-life crisis is an internal storm of self-doubt that generates daunting realizations like these:

> "I've already lived half my life, yet I don't know who I am, or who I was meant to become."

> "I don't know where I'm going, or what I was meant to do, or why."

Mid-life crisis is like waking up on a small boat in a storm, though mid-lifers' reactions vary. Some just go back to sleep. Others jump over the side, out of marriages, out of old work, into new relationships, new jobs, new geography, new lifestyles. Most just hang on to the tiller until the storm eventually subsides. The storm can rage for years.

A very clever movie, "The Truman Show", portrays one man's mid-life crisis. Truman (played by Jim Carrey) lives a picture-perfect suburban life in Seahaven, a model coastal town. Unknown to Truman, hidden cameras have recorded his every moment since birth, and broadcast them live to a captivated worldwide TV audience. "The Truman Show" is the world's most watched TV production.

Seahaven is an artificial town bordering an artificial sea, all inside a gigantic domed television studio. The dome-contained environment is entirely controlled by Christof (played by Ed Harris), the Truman Show's tyrannical director, who programs its artificial weather and commands its artificial sun, moon, planets and stars. Christof's most memorable line is, "Cue the Sun!" Everyone Truman has ever met is an actor, even his wife, who crossed her fingers during their wedding vows. Each actor is fitted with tiny earphones through which Christof dictates lines and issues stage directions.

Inevitably, Truman begins to suspect his life has been a charade, and fantasizes about travel to Fiji. Though deathly afraid of water, he flees Seahaven in a small sailboat. Christof orders up an artificial storm to foil Truman's escape. When the sea calms, the sailboat bumps against the outer shell of the gigantic dome. Dramatically, Truman locates a door leading to the real world outside Seahaven, whose existence he's begun to suspect.

Mid-life crisis can play havoc in the workplace. Confused and hurting, it's common to blame bosses and co-workers for whipping up your internal storm. Change jobs, and the storm follows you. Seek escape by working longer and harder, having more children, and the storm intensifies. The fortunate have understanding families, bosses, colleagues and friends who help them ride it out.

Tethered by golden handcuffs—high salaries, benefits and perks—the family business can seem like the Seahaven dome to restless younger generation members. They can escape the dome, but not the family. Business families need to understand these internal storms, and help their Trumans hang on to the tiller.

19

Searching for Inside Talent: Get Expert Input from Outside

It's challenging to choose new leaders from inside your organization.

It's more difficult to choose them from inside your family.

Either way, you're too close to be objective. That's when outside expertise can make the difference between a good choice and an unfortunate one.

Roger, a brilliant young entrepreneur, couldn't decide whether to hire his older brother, Todd. Roger's company was growing very fast. He was working night and day, neglecting his family and his health. Roger badly needed a top notch executive vice-president.

Brother Todd worked for a much larger company in the same industry, where his career opportunities there were limited. Todd had technical know-how and good people skills. Roger trusted Todd and thought they could be a good team.

However, when Roger floated the idea by his board, he got a surprise. "Don't hire your brother!" advised one director. "If your brother's your number two, you'll have trouble hiring other highly talented people you really need. They won't want to work for both of you. Besides, what if it doesn't work out with your brother?"

Roger called me a few days before he and Todd were leaving for a week-long trip together. They would have lots of time to talk. I cautioned Roger against making an early offer. Todd might accept it out of loyalty to Roger, but later regret his decision. Instead, why not just encourage Todd to talk? As a listener, Roger could focus on Todd as a potential leader in his company, and likely learn if Todd was interested in making a change.

When Roger returned from their trip, he was all smiles. "Did you hire your brother?" I asked. "No, he isn't the man for the job, and he doesn't want it anyway." I pressed: "Did you invite him?" "No, and I'm glad I didn't. It would have been hard for him to turn me down. I think we both avoided an unfortunate situation."

So with Todd out of the picture, how will Roger locate his critical number two executive? "I'll take a closer look at my key inside people. If none of them measures up, I'll hire an executive search firm", he said.

I suggested an alternative. "Why not hire the search firm to evaluate your inside candidates? Have the search firm test and interview them as though they were outsiders." Had brother Todd been a candidate, I would have suggested the same process. Roger was making his most important hire. He was too close to his inside candidates, and much too close to his brother. He needed objective expert outside input.

I don't agree with Roger's director who counseled against hiring Todd just because he was a brother. Some brother teams have worked business miracles. I might have introduced Roger and Todd to brothers who have been hugely successful in business together, and to two other brothers who had recently asked a third brother to leave their family company.

Lots of unfortunate inside hires and promotions could be avoided by objective input from outside search firms or career counselors. Outside professionals spot talent and weaknesses, and assess motivation and fit. The pros can help companies avoid mistakes, and help business families avoid heartaches.

Part Three

Financial Estate Planning for the Relational Estate

Some Guideposts and Warning Signs:

25.　Most of us who have estate plans can't tell you what's in them. We thought we understood at the time we signed the documents, but somehow that has slipped away.

26.　Too much estate planning takes place in secret. Too many dear ones are taken for granted or by surprise.

27.　Our world is awash with advice, some expensive, some free, some profound, some loony, some dangerous. How do we sort it out?

28.　Suppose you're making a choice that could change the unfolding story of your life—a story-changing choice. Will you make that story-changing choice alone, or share the choosing, or let someone else choose for you?

29.　Some choose with their heads and hope their hearts will follow along. Head choosers may counsel you too choose "unemotionally", but I don't.

30.　Conventional wisdom: "The number one opportunity for an estate plan to go wrong occurs when parents tie the children to the same asset or when they require the children to do a job together as a group."

31.　In almost every case of ill-shared inheritances and stuck business families I encounter, family members were *under prepared* for the acute interpersonal stresses associated with being joined at the wallet.

32. Relational estates are very high maintenance. For wealthy families who want to remediate some neglected family skills, a family council can offer the needed impetus and structure.

33. In my experience, a common obstacle to succession in a family business is the senior generation's unspoken fear of impoverishing themselves in old age.

34. Aging clients want what eluded poor King Lear: they want financial security, attentive health care, a connected family at peace, and a positive legacy by which they are remembered.

35. Medieval alchemists failed to turn lead into gold. Wealthy twenty-first century parents fear a reverse alchemy. Will their children transmute inherited gold into leaden lives—hollow, shallow, self-absorbed, indolent, meaningless, wasted?

36. New wealth seems more fearful of wealth corrupting their children than old wealth, and thus are more controlling of their children than old wealth.

37. Isn't it ironic that it's time to teach our children before we know ourselves? At best we grow up along with them and we learn together with them. It's called parenting.

20

Beclouded by Croakspeak? Take Charge!

Most of us who have estate plans can't tell you what's in them. We thought we understood at the time we signed the documents, but somehow that has slipped away.

Granted, estate planning can be complicated, especially for the well-heeled. And it's not much fun to think about the financial fallout from our croaking.

But that's not why we forgot. We forgot because we didn't take charge. We abdicated our financial immortality to hired wizards who beclouded our memories with croakspeak.

Spoken croakspeak assumes you can't bear to talk about your own death,

"If something happens ..."

Written croakspeak sounds like a wizard's incantation,

"I give, grant, bequeath, devise, set over and enfeoff ..."

Arise, all ye who would rather sit for a root canal than discuss the financial consequences of your death. Take charge!

Begin with three sheets of blank paper. Forget all you know, or think you know about estate planning, or have heard at the beauty parlor or the golf course. Make your mind as blank as the paper.

On one sheet write down who you *really* want to get what when you die.

On a second sheet, write down what you *really* think those who get it will do with it.

On the third sheet, write down what you *really* want to do or accomplish between today and the day you croak.

At the very first meeting with your wizard, and before the cave becomes beclouded with croakspeak, produce these three sheets of paper. Insist that you and your wizard start with what you have written down. Then let your wizard do his or her croakspeak thing.

Your wizard is expert at making sure that what you want to happen—post croak—actually comes to pass. But your wizard doesn't know what you want unless you say. And unless you say it very clearly, your wizard will get preoccupied with saving croak taxes and croakspeak syntax ... all at the risk of casting your three sheets to the winds.

Here are three more suggestions about taking charge:

One: Ask your wizard how the proposed estate plan will *really* play out in your life and in the lives of those dear ones who will get your stuff; how the plan will *really* affect your most important relationships, and theirs; in other words, the plan's impact on your relational estate.

Two: Ask if those dear ones who will get your stuff can come and listen to your wizard's explanation.

Three: Do One and Two before you sign anything.

Do all this while you are still healthy and influential with those dear ones. Ask for their reactions and suggested changes to your wizard's proposed plan.

Too much estate planning takes place in secret.

Too many dear ones are taken for granted or by surprise.

In secret we leave our dear ones what we think they *ought* to want in ways we think they *ought* to want to get it. But we don't involve them.

No amount of croakspeak can substitute for candid conversations with our dear ones.

Ask them, talk with them, get their input, then decide and have the wizard do *your* thing.

Yes, those conversations could lead to tears. After all, the topic is your death. And that's hard for you and for them. But not nearly as hard as taking dear ones for granted or by surprise after you're gone.

Don't become beclouded by croakspeak.

Take charge of your estate plan!

21

Taking Good Advice: Story-Changing Choices

My client owned a coffee company. Twenty years ago, his pricey experts forecast that baby boomers wouldn't be coffee drinkers and would never buy bottled drinking water at soft drink prices.

Our world is awash with advice, some expensive, some free, some profound, some loony, some dangerous. How do we sort it out? How do we choose which advice to follow, and which to ignore? Here's some advice about taking advice.

Step No. 1: Do you need help with a choice? Or do you just need someone to listen to your story and share your feelings about it? Do you want the other person to empathize or to strategize? Be clear at the outset whether you *want* advice. She could begin: "I'm not asking for advice right now, I just want to ventilate about this." Or he could ask: "Do you want me to listen or do you want me to fix it?" Asking someone to listen invites empathy. Asking someone to help you choose, invites advice. Be clear.

Step No. 2: Suppose you're making a choice that could change the unfolding story of your life—a story-changing choice. Some examples: to have a child or another child, to change jobs or locales, to stay or to split with your partner, to undergo major surgery, to write a will.

Will you make that story-changing choice alone, or share the choosing, or let someone else choose for you? Some people of faith hand off story-changing choices to a Higher Power.

How might your choice affect others' life stories? Should you check in with them before choosing? Ask for their input, if not their advice? "Suppose I take a job abroad?" "What if I name you executor of my estate?" Having a child is a clear shared choice. So is moving away if you're leaving together. You may be cool with someone else making a story-changing choice for you. "If you want another child, we'll have one." A caution: if you let others choose for you, you forfeit the right to complain or to second-guess their choices.

Step No. 3: Are you qualified to make a story-changing choice wisely? Or do you need professional advice from someone with special knowledge—a physician, lawyer, psychologist, accountant, or clergy? It's a mistake to delegate your *choice* to experts. Expert advisors don't want to substitute their judgment for yours. They want *you* to make informed choices supplemented by *their* expertise. And that's the way it should be. It's *your* body, *your* money, *your* relationships, *your* soul. If your expert advisor tries to make choices for you, I'd get a second opinion.

Step No. 4: Choose timely. Don't rush, but don't dawdle either. What events need to fall into place before you choose? What do you need to know beforehand? Establish a sensible deadline for choosing, and don't be afraid to change it. Unmade choices can increase your anxiety level, disturb your sleep, sour your disposition. Resist well-meaning friends who detect your discomfort and push you to choose prematurely. You risk overlooking something important that only the passage of time can reveal. Likewise, resist well-meaning friends who would lull you into procrastinating.

Step No. 5: Don't discount your feelings. Some choose with their heads and hope their hearts will follow along. Head choosers may counsel you to choose "unemotionally", but I don't. Emotions can play a huge part in how and when you choose. If you resist choosing unless or until you *feel* right about your choice, that's probably OK.

Step No. 6: Sometimes you can't choose—you're disabled or deceased. That's why you name guardians for your minor children, executors, trustees. That's why you give powers of attorney so others can manage your finances or make your heath care decisions. Some families fight furiously about what a loved one "intended" after they're gone. Those who will choose on your behalf need to know all they can about how you would choose—if you could. Brief them thoroughly.

Rejecting that expensive expert advice, my client has sold oceans of coffee and bottled water over the last twenty years.

It costs you nothing to reject my advice about taking advice.

22

Sibling-Shared Inheritances: Red Flags, Yellow Flags ... or Green Flags?

In his "Children in a Rowboat" articles, Atlanta attorney Robert Edge perpetuates a popular notion among estate planners about sibling-shared inheritance:

> The number one opportunity for an estate plan to go wrong occurs when parents tie the children to the same asset or when they require the children to do a job together as a group. This can happen when a surviving parent names several children to serve as executors of a complicated estate, to run the family business, to share an expensive house, or even to distribute assets of the family foundation.

> Imagine loading the children into a rowboat on a big lake and requiring them to agree on one destination when their rowboat can go in only one direction, no matter how many passengers it holds.

> There may not be many truisms in estate planning, but there is one goal that has prime importance for almost all clients: they do not want a legacy to result in their children avoiding one another.

> Plans that require children to agree among themselves when their parents are both gone are simply fraught with danger. Don't we owe the client at least a yellow flag, or sometimes a red one, when a suggestion is made to put the children in the same rowboat as fiduciaries or beneficiaries?

Thus the conventional wisdom is that children in a rowboat fly a red flag ... or at least a yellow flag. I suspect Bob Edge speaks from long experience with contentious sibling heirs. Mark Twain's wry remark comes to mind:

> "You never really know someone until you share an inheritance with them."

Contentious sibling rivalries don't turn themselves into lawsuits. The legal system is an arch enabler. Elsewhere I wrote:

> A war-like 'win-lose' radical individualism permeates the law's current approach to all human relationships, whether commercial or personal. The adversary process assumes that all relationships will ultimately fail, whereupon every individual will need a lawyer to protect him or her from everyone else, even from family.

> No doubt *some* sibling relationships would be better served by separated inheritances. It's better to sell their parents' vacation home than to suffer the ongoing ordeal of fights over access and fussing over maintenance. But for other siblings, the very sharing of their parents' vacation home reinforces relationships, preserves memories, continues to connect them.

How does an advisor determine whether clients' children are good risks to share an inheritance—red flag or green flag? Does the advisor raise the issue of shared inheritance as a neutral, yellow flag perhaps, or reveal the advisor's bias based on some bitter past experiences with other families of ill-sharing siblings—i.e. red flag, "children in a rowboat"?

Consider other "rowboat" implications. Notwithstanding advisors' red flags, lots of fifty-fifty partnerships work out just fine. That most prevalent fifty-fifty partnership—marriage—is also risky. But just because half of the marriages entered this year will end in divorce, neither Bob Edge nor I would discourage formation of marital partnerships, though both might counsel caution and a close look at prenuptial agreements. Is the couple *prepared* to work through the stresses of a wealthy marriage?

In almost every case of ill-shared inheritances and stuck family businesses I encounter, family members were *under prepared* for the acute interpersonal stresses associated with being joined at the wallet. Family skills have been neglected and need work.

Here's a partial listing of specific family skills I think necessary to successfully share an inheritance or a business:

- Habits of comfortable communication.

- Clear boundaries between personal independence and family interdependence.

- Rivalry management.

- Accepting differences.

- A capacity to differentiate between thinking and feeling, and a vocabulary for both.

- A willingness to forgive.

- Healthy emotional engagement.

- The ability to listen without judging.

- An understanding that encourages individual family members to speak their own minds, but discourages them from trying to speak others' minds.

Why not share this checklist of family skills with clients contemplating sibling-shared inheritances? Or better yet, suggest that the clients share the checklist with their children? In my view, broad family feedback is the best indicator of whether a sibling-shared inheritance makes sense. Further, it's helpful to ascertain if the potentially sharing siblings *like* each other, and whether *they* favor or oppose the prospect of shared inheritance.

If family feedback indicates deficiencies in family skills, or yellow—or red flags to shared inheritance, the family's relational estate may need work. Relational estates are very high maintenance. For wealthy families who want to remediate some neglected family skills, a family council can offer the needed impetus and structure.

In the military, we trained in heavy oceangoing lifeboats, six facing aft heaving hard on the oars, a coxswain manning the tiller, barking the cadence. A successful family council is no recreational rowboat on a pond. It's more like a lifeboat with everyone pulling an oar to keep family and fortune afloat in sometimes heavy seas. A successful family council can be the family's lifeboat.

23

King Lear Fear: What Aging Clients Really Want

King Lear, Shakespeare's most tragic character, had a crazy estate plan.

Lear would abdicate his throne, and then divide his lands among whichever of his three daughters flattered him most. One loyal daughter refused to play the flattery game so Lear banished her. The other two poured on the flattery, took his lands, and then threw him out.

Upon discovering both were having an affair with the same man, one of the flatter daughters poisoned the other, then stabbed herself to death. Meanwhile, the loyal daughter was executed by mistake. Lear now broken, abandoned and demented, began to converse with mice.

King Lear's sorry end personifies what aging clients most dread. Lear died broke, sick and senile, his family a train wreck, his legacy to be forever remembered as a vain buffoon. Aging clients want what eluded poor Lear: financial security, attentive health care, a connected family at peace, and a positive legacy by which they are remembered.

Financial Security. An aging client confides, "I'm afraid of running out of money before I die." Estate advisors should first address this primal fear of aged impoverishment. Once relieved of this lifetime concern, the client can focus on avoiding death taxes. Some aging clients *do* run out of money before they die because, like Lear, they've improvidently passed on property prematurely.

In my experience, a common obstacle to succession in family business is the senior generation's unspoken fear of impoverishing themselves in old age. The younger generation are unproven managers whose plans may be as crazy as Lear's. Or the senior generation's plan may be crazy too, e.g. continuing huge unearned salaries, perks and benefits for life—a long term liability the company can ill-afford.

Attentive Health Care. "Who will take care of me when I can no longer care for myself?" The family is the primary support group for its aging members. I urge families to discuss carefully how they will cope with members' inevitable declining health. A health care power of attorney and living will are important of course, but not nearly enough. Who will convince an aging parent to give up driving? Who will assure that the physician has been understood, that prescriptions are taken as directed, that good nutrition and exercise are available and encouraged, that the retirement facility lives up to its bargain? Health concerns in old age are not only a family concern, but a whole family undertaking. Lear's loyal daughter suffered acute caregiver burnout while her flatter sisters cavorted.

Family Peace. "I'm not going to finance a family fight when I die!" declared a very thoughtful client. In the vain pursuit of flattery, poor Lear did just that. It was shear buffoonery to stage a flattery contest with huge prizes that overheated murderous sibling rivalries. Surely Lear didn't assume such a competition could *promote* family peace.

In my experience, the estate planning community is thrown off balance by contentious families, e.g. by adult sibling rivalries running out of control. Tax avoidance and financial products seldom provide an antidote for such hostilities. Nor does estate planning in secret, where parents are encouraged to leave children what they ought to want without asking or forewarning them.

Fortunately, intergenerational estate planning is catching on. The family as a whole, parents and children, givers and receivers, talk openly about what the parents have and what it's worth, who would like to inherit it, and how the inheritance should be managed. Along the way they discuss the roles of executors, powers of attorney over parents' assets, health care powers, and whether Mom would *really* be the best choice for those fiduciary offices. Quite often Mom discourages her appointment, further suggesting that others speak to Dad about no longer driving when the time comes.

Senior clients need the comfort of family peace during their later years. After they are gone, they want their estates to be enjoyed by peaceable survivors whose recollections and reminders of their parents' largess are themselves, peaceful memories.

"How Will I Be Remembered?" Beginning in their sixties, increasingly in their seventies, and overwhelmingly in their eighties, senior clients are concerned about their "legacy"—how they will be remembered. Dad might not get much professional encouragement about leaving a legacy of peace to warring children. "Give it to charity if they can't get along" counsels one advisor. "Tie it up in trust" advises another.

Dad doesn't want to "finance a family fight". If necessary, he'll reluctantly play the role of peacemaker, and won't mind being remembered as such. He fantasizes about his children reminiscing after his funeral:

"Dad didn't want his money to divide us."

"He stayed on us until we buried the hatchet, or at least locked it away."

"I guess he was right that parenting never ends."

"In his eighties and still dishing out tough love!"

"I've got to admire him for that."

Lear's loopy plan—land-for-flattery—was doomed from the outset. He failed as a king and as a father with such colossal grandiosity that Shakespeare immortalized his folly. Aging clients want what eluded poor Lear: financial security, attentive health care, a connected family at peace, and a positive legacy by which they are remembered.

24

Controlling Kids with Money: Incentive Trusts Rarely Work

The following is from my book, "Raising Rich Kids":

> Medieval alchemists failed to turn lead into gold. Wealthy twenty-first century parents fear a reverse alchemy. Will their children transmute inherited gold into leaden lives—hollow, shallow, self-absorbed, addicted, indolent, meaningless, wasted?

Several years ago a front page Wall Street Journal story reported that star pitcher Tom Glavine, then of the Atlanta Braves, had created incentive trusts for his three sons. So long as a son remained married to a stay-at-home mom, there would be trust distributions; otherwise, none. At the 2003 annual meeting of the American College of Trust and Estate Counsel an expert panel discussed the pros and cons of these so-called incentive trusts.

Many incentive trusts authorize distributions equal to the beneficiary's earned income i.e. "earn a dollar, get a dollar." Others reward educational achievement or the avoidance of alcohol or drugs. One parent instructed the trustee of his chronically late children to make trust distributions only to those who showed up at the appointed place on time.

Incentive trusts seem most popular with the new entrepreneurial wealthy who grew up with middle class values and had no experience with "trust babies." They fondly quote Warren Buffet: "I want my children to have enough to do anything but not enough to do nothing." New wealth seems more controlling of their children than old wealth.

The ACTEC panelists suggested that external standards of behavior ignore the more important goal of fortifying the beneficiary internally. The incentive trust imposes outside control instead of encouraging the beneficiary to develop internal controls, emphasizing outward conformity over personal growth and maturity.

Incentive trusts curtail trustee discretion over distributions by substituting objective standards for beneficiaries' behavior. "Incentivizing" behavior essentially supplants the traditional trustee-beneficiary relationship. Instead of functioning as mentor, model and coach, the trustee becomes a mere referee.

The ACTEC panel distinguished trust distributions that honor "benchmarks of maturity" such as graduation, marriage, the birth of children, etc. from incentive trusts that reward what the child would not otherwise do. They were particularly concerned with incentive trusts' narrow definitions of desirable and undesirable conduct and their failure to define larger family values and principles.

All agreed that incentive trusts may be useful for incorrigible children who might otherwise be disinherited by parents who have done all they can without success. Disappointed parents—and the major religions—still hold out hope that the most wayward children may yet change their ways.

In lieu of incentive trusts, the ACTEC panelists encouraged cooperative ventures such as family limited partnerships and family charities. Here, the beneficiaries are involved, receive information and participate in decisions even though they may not control the enterprise. Inside the loop with their parents, they collaborate on prudent investing and the financial expression of family values.

One ACTEC panelist advocated a "productivity trust" with a mission statement that defines what the family wants its members to do and be, with guidelines towards accomplishing those ends. A trust advisory committee meets frequently with beneficiaries, freely sharing information. The greater collaboration and sharing between beneficiaries and trustees, the less likely the tensions between them.

I have long questioned the wisdom of incentive trusts and applaud this thoughtful ACTEC panel whose combined estate planning experience reaches the same conclusion. Active collaboration between parents and children on family limited partnerships and family charities can reinforce those vital internal gyroscopes that help guide children through a murky world.

Near the end of "Raising Rich Kids", the narrator talks with a psychologist, who observes:

> "Isn't it ironic that it's time to teach our children before we know ourselves. At best we grow up along with them and we learn together with them. It's called parenting."

> "So we and our children search together for answers to their money questions?"

"I think so."

> "Aren't those the best answers, the answers you discover together? Inside answers instead of outside answers."

Part Four

Pursuing Family Happiness

Some Guideposts and Warning Signs:

38. Despite a huge growth in affluence since WWII, American levels of happiness have remained essentially flat.

39. Neurophysiologists confirm a correlation between happiness and the development of antibodies, resistance to heart disease, diabetes and upper respiratory infections.

40. One thing is sure: all of us want to become happy and stay happy. Some very prominent psychologists—who understand the human psyche best—are trying to help us do just that.

41. As he wrote the Declaration of Independence, I think Thomas Jefferson intended to implant a revolutionary survival skill into the public conscience of his new country: a duty to pursue *others'* happiness.

42. Lots of people claim to be pursing my happiness these days. It would be nice to believe them, to wallow in their promises, to buy their stuff, and just ignore the needs of those whose happiness Jefferson admonished me to pursue.

43. The new positive psychology teaches that the likeliest route to our own authentic happiness lies in pursuing the happiness of others.

44. Happy work is emotionally and intellectually stimulating, fulfils our need to feel useful to others, creates meaning in our lives.

45. The saddest cases I see are people who feel locked into high-paying but unhappy work by "golden handcuffs". The fun is long gone, the drudgery is ever present, the responsibility is unrelenting.

46. Friendships contribute more to our physical and mental health than money, fame, or success.

47. Friendship is an adult version of children's play.

48. Friend-making and friendship keeping have become survival skills.

49. Friendship is both art and skill. Friendship is a cornerstone of human happiness.

50. Family discord doesn't necessarily mean the family is unhappy. Nor does relief from current discord necessarily restore them to happiness.

51. The source of family discord lies somewhere inside their relational estate. That's also where you'll find their self-mediation skills, such as they are.

52. Some self-mediation skills are those same skills that created the family wealth. Too often, however, equally important self-mediation skills are left underdeveloped or neglected. The very self-mediation skills they neglect could be the keys to richer, happier family lives.

53. Comfortable communication, non-judgmental listening, speaking for one-self but not for others, emotional engagement, rivalry management, separated thinking and feeling, willingness to forgive, accepting differences—these are not just self-mediation skills. They are relational gateways to family enrichment.

25

Happiness: A New Science?

The Declaration of Independence enshrines "the pursuit of happiness" as Americans' inalienable right. But what is happiness? Who is happy? And how does one pursue it? A recent issue of *Time* explored recent "happiness research" that may provide some answers.

Imagine a "happiness-misery index" calibrated from minus five (despair) up to plus five (bliss). Modern psychology has been preoccupied with misery—that dark realm of mental illness. Historically, psychotherapists' goal has been to move miserable people up the misery index towards zero. In the process, they have relieved oceans of human suffering.

Until recently, few serious psychologists focused on the happiness-misery index north of zero. What makes the human heart sing? A new "positive psychology" is exploring happiness—optimism, positive emotions, healthy character traits, our experience of well-being ... fun! Happiness research recalls some old lyrics:

> "You've got to accentuate the positive, eliminate the negative, don't mess with Mr. In-between".

Happiness researchers learned that neither wealth nor income raises our sense of satisfaction with life, once basic needs are met. Nor does education or a high IQ. Virtues of the head—curiosity and love of learning—are less tied to happiness than virtues of the heart—kindness, gratitude, and capacity for love. Youth isn't a factor either. Older persons are more consistently satisfied and less prone to dark moods. Married persons are more content than singles. Some 900 Texas women reported their happiest activities, in order of importance, to be: sex, socializing, relaxing, praying and eating.

No one maintains a constant state of bliss. The happiest of us are down at least 10% of the time; the miserable are elevated about the same amount. Even the happiest are brought low for extended periods of time by loss of spouse or loss of job. The sources of one's capacity for happiness seem to be roughly 50% genetic and 50% the cumulative effect of "slings and arrows" i.e. life experience.

As one moves upscale on the happiness-misery index, physical well-being improves. Neurophysiologists confirm a correlation between happiness and the development of antibodies, resistance to heart disease, diabetes and upper respiratory infections. It's correspondingly unhealthy downscale. Those who are anxious and depressed are more susceptible to disease.

Laughter—"evolution's whoopee cushion"—exercises the heart and elevates our mood. Men are the leading laugh getters; women are the leading laughers.

Despite a huge growth in affluence since WWII, American levels of happiness have remained essentially flat. But clinical depression is three to ten times as prevalent today as two generations ago. One in fifteen Americans experience an episode of major depression e.g. can't get out of bed.

Any suggested correlation between wealth and happiness is thus suspect. Of course being poor can cause depression, but we know that. One researcher concludes that after income exceeds $50,000 annually, happiness and affluence decouple. Further income increases don't drive up the happiness index. The Forbes 400 wealthiest are only slightly happier than the public at large. Moreover, as Americans move up the economic ladder, they almost immediately stop feeling grateful for their elevated circumstances and focus on what they still don't have. Whatever their income level, Americans believe they need more to live well. Those who anticipate they'll get still more seem even happier.

A psychologist father-son team administered a "subjective well-being" questionnaire to members of many cultures around the world, with some surprising results. Latin Americans (along with Americans) are among the happiest, while East Asians (Japan, China, South Korea) are among the least happy, with somber Lithuanians and Russians at the bottom.

British Economist Sir Richard Layard praises the American Declaration of Independence. Public policy should, says Sir Richard, be judged by how government increases human happiness and alleviates human misery. Layard credits focus on public happiness with much of the social progress accomplished over the last two centuries. Building stable and happy families, communities and workplaces deserve to be very high public priorities.

Psychologist Martin Seligman, a founder of positive psychology, became interested in happiness research because he had nothing further to offer therapy clients who neared zero on the happiness-misery index. I felt a similar frustration as a mediator: once the family wealth dispute was resolved, then what? How does a once-contentious family refocus on family happiness so long obscured by their wranglings?

Is this new approach to happiness just another smiley-face pop psychology? Or are the positive psychologists on to something? One thing is sure: all of us want to become happy and stay happy. Some very prominent psychologists—who understand the human psyche best—are trying to help us do just that.

Let's listen to what they have to say.

26

A Survival Skill: Pursuing Others' Happiness

According to anthropologists, human brain architecture has changed little during the past 250,000 years. Our brains still carry strong primal survival circuits, some positive, some negative.

Our negative survival circuits are defensive, win-lose, fight or run away. Win-lose circuits generate negative emotions such as fear, sadness, anger, bitterness and loss, all necessary to avert danger, all very unpleasant feelings.

Our positive survival circuits are creative, win-win. They prompt us to have children, to nurture them and each other, to build, enhance, improve, enjoy. They generate positive emotions that give us a sense of well being, make us happy. Positive emotions are fun!

During the first 247,000 years in our modern brains, we were savages. Negative survival emotions prevailed. Only over the past 3000 years, has humankind begun the jerky transition from savages, to barbarians, then to civilized people … at least more or less. Only during the past 3000 years has civilization's win-win begun to edge out savagery's win-lose. Only over the past 3000 years has life offered us more time off from survival to explore happiness.

Positive psychologists view happiness a cluster of positive emotions about our past, our present, and our future. Happiness about our past generates satisfaction, pride, contentment, serenity. We're happy about having raised children, even if we weren't always happy while bringing them up. Happiness about our future generates optimism, hope, trust, confidence, faith. Our children may be a handful today, but we're working hard to offer them future opportunities that didn't come our way.

Surveyors asked 900 Texas women what made them happiest. They responded in order of importance: sex, socializing, relaxing, praying and eating. Their answers reflect widespread confusion about what makes us "right now happy". Positive psychologists identify two kinds of "right now happy": pleasure and gratification. Pleasure is sensual and momentary, like a glass of good wine. Gratification is more practiced and learned, like a round of golf, a good book, a warm conversation with a close friend.

If you're confused about happiness, join the club. Over the past 3000 years, much has been said about human happiness, much of it conflicting. The Old Norse word *happ* meant "favored by the gods". It survives in modern English words such as happy, mishap, happenstance, even perhaps. In the ancient world, happiness was just good luck, like winning the lottery. No, said ancient Greek philosophers, we can achieve happiness by right thinking. Early Christian theologians saw happiness, not as cerebral, but emotional and ecstatic though reserved for the faithful in the after-life. Jeremy Bentham said happiness on earth is the greatest good for the greatest number. A legion of gloomy intellectuals, including psychiatrist Sigmund Freud, concluded that happiness is an illusion and thus unattainable. Today's TV commercials promise happiness if we buy the right stuff. Cartoon smiley faces wish us a nice day.

In the Declaration of Independence, Thomas Jefferson inscribed the "pursuit of happiness" as an inalienable right. Jefferson enjoyed books, wine, music, travel, good conversation, and most of all, his home at Monticello. But that's not what Jefferson meant by happiness. With those words, I think Jefferson intended to implant a revolutionary survival skill into the public conscience of his new country: a duty to pursue *others'* happiness.

Pursuing others' happiness isn't always fun. And there's no "Easy Button". Jefferson's pleasure was interrupted by years away from Monticello in public service that was anything but fun or easy. Raising an infant nation, like raising our own children, could be downright unpleasant, exhausting, discouraging, require sacrifice.

Lots of people claim to be pursuing my happiness these days. It would be nice to believe them, to wallow in their promises, to buy their stuff, and just ignore the needs of those whose happiness Jefferson admonished me to pursue.

Doggone it, Mr. Jefferson, pursuing happiness is so inconvenient!

27

Pursuing Happiness: Why Not?

What did Thomas Jefferson mean by "the pursuit of happiness" when he penned it into the Declaration of Independence as an inalienable right? In a recent Wall Street Journal column, Darren McMahon explores this curious but carefully chosen phrase.

"The pursuit of happiness" peppered eighteenth century sermons. God delighted to see his creatures happy. There was far less brooding about original sin than in earlier times. As the not-so-pious Benjamin Franklin opined, "wine is living proof that god loves us and wants us to be happy."

Two years before the Declaration of Independence, the First Continental Congress had complained of the king's intrusions into colonists' "life, liberty and *property*". Of course property could bring pleasure, but property was not what Jefferson said or meant by "happiness". From Aristotle and Cicero, along with Locke and Newton, Jefferson learned "that happiness was the great goal of the well-lived life, achieved through discipline, self-sacrifice and reasoned moderation", writes Professor McMahon.

Glittering TV goddess Paris Hilton take note: Jeffersonian happiness is founded not in momentary pleasure, but rather upon virtue. Virtue at its highest is working for the public good. Jefferson foresaw that independent Americans would discover their own happiness by pursuing the happiness of others. As Professor McMahon emphasizes, "no 18th century Founder, whether a Christian or classicist, or cultivator of simple pleasures would have disagreed."

Martin Seligman, the a founder of positive psychology, was astonished to discover that among 200 cultures and traditions over the past 3000 years, there is virtual agreement as to six anchor virtues:

1. Wisdom and knowledge

2. Courage

3. Love and humanity

4. Justice

5. Temperance and self-restraint (balance and self-discipline)

6. Transcendence and spirituality (allegiance to something outside and greater than ourselves).

Seligman's research further identified twenty-four positive character traits most closely associated with attainment of those six anchor virtues. At least twelve of these positive character traits involve pursuing the happiness of others.

1. Curiosity

2. Love of learning

3. Judgment, critical thinking, open-mindedness

4. Ingenuity, originality, practical intelligence

5. Social intelligence, personal intelligence, emotional intelligence ("street smarts")

6. Perspective

7. Valor and bravery

8. Perseverance, industry, diligence

9. Integrity, genuineness, honesty

10. Kindness and generosity

11. Loving and allowing oneself to be loved

12. Citizenship, teamwork, loyalty

13. Fairness and equity

14. Leadership

15. Self-control

16. Prudence, discretion, caution

17. Humility and modesty

18. Appreciation of beauty and excellence

19. Gratitude

20. Hope, optimism, future-mindedness

21. Spirituality, a sense of purpose, faith

22. Forgiveness and mercy

23. Playfulness and humor

24. Zest, passion, enthusiasm

Positive psychology teaches that the likeliest route to our own authentic happiness lies in pursuing the happiness of others.

Mr. Jefferson, meet Professor Seligman.

So long, Paris Hilton.

28

Happy Work: More Fun than Fun!

"Work is much more fun than fun!" exclaimed actor-writer Noel Coward.

Happy work is better work. Happy workers get better evaluations, more promotions, make more money.

Happy work offers more than money. The workplace is a great place to meet people, establish important relationships. One in four meets their spouse at work. Happy work is emotionally and intellectually stimulating, fulfils our need to feel useful to others, creates meaning in our lives. After all, we work the greater part of our waking hours.

Psychologist Mihaly Csikszentmihayli says we can become so absorbed in happy work that time stands still for us, a timeless experience he calls "flow". Ah, but isn't work a curse? Isn't work our congenital punishment for Adam's and Eve's apple-eating in the Garden of Eden? Aren't we supposed to be *un*happy at work? If work is fun, isn't "flow" somehow sinful?

A client of mine is a third generation funeral director. He experiences "flow" as he restores a face in preparation for the family's last viewing. Surgeons report "flow" while performing operations. Surgery is intellectually stimulating; to help healing is emotionally satisfying. Less dramatic work, no less dignified, can generate "flow"—the caring hearse driver, the gentle nurse's aid.

Time was when back pain was the main cause for employee absenteeism. Today it's depression and anxiety caused largely by unhappy work: long hours, fierce deadlines, office politics, harassing or bullying managers. Job satisfaction is a strong indicator of how satisfied we are with ourselves.

We are increasingly defined by the work we do. If my work is miserable, am I not a miserable person as well?

So why continue a miserable job? Many say we endure unhappy work for the money, or status, or to pursue a calling. But if you're in unhappy work, ask yourself: Do I want the job I have? Do I know what job I really want? Does my job reflect who I really am? If your answer indicates a change, then next time find a new job that matches your skills, that's worthwhile, that gives you some control over your work. See a really good career counselor before your next job change. But keep your perspective: the unhappiest people of all are the unemployed.

Next to adequate pay and acceptable working conditions, two intangible factors contribute most to happy work: a sense of accomplishment and being recognized for what we accomplish. Smart managers praise good work publicly, and make it fun!

As I mediate disputes about family wealth and family business, I get to watch hugely successful entrepreneurs lead their employees. Entrepreneurs are high energy, hard workers, demanding bosses. Most are both feared and beloved by their employees. They are tough but sensitive. They inspire fierce loyalty and demand grim devotion. Yet entrepreneurs generate a contagious excitement. They're having fun and it's fun to work for them—if you can stand the pace.

The saddest cases I see are people who feel locked into high-paying but unhappy work by "golden handcuffs". They have children in college, high house payments, an expensive upwards spiraling lifestyle. Some are physicians, lawyers, stockbrokers, corporate executives. Some are entrepreneurs' children who feel stuck in the family business. The fun is long gone, the drudgery is ever present, the responsibility is unrelenting.

A confession: happy work fascinates me because I worked unhappily for so many years before the fun began. I viewed my unhappy work—a miscast lawyer—as a macho inheritance from Adam and Eve. Work wasn't supposed to be fun; work was to be endured. How sad. How sad it was to herd contentious families through the dismal swamps of litigation. But now, as a mediator, my job is to help them bypass the courthouse. Peacemaking is fun!

For this recovering lawyer, happy work is too good to be true.

29

Friendships:
They Die But They Don't

A recent photo of President George W. Bush and Saudi Crown Prince Abdullah attracted wide attention. President and Prince were holding hands. This may have turned heads in Texas, but the photo sent a message of cordiality across the Middle East where public hand-holding is a common sign of male friendship.

Consider how much your happiness depends on friends. Friendships contribute more to our physical and mental health than money, fame, or success. Friendship is extremely valuable, but very inexpensive. Unlike family, neighbors or coworkers, we can choose our friends without the complications of romance or kinship. Friends know our faults and weaknesses but choose to like us anyway.

We unwind with friends. Friendship is an adult version of children's play. Fun, joy, mimicry, teasing and laughter are all parts of friendship. We laugh thirty times more often with friends than when alone.

Friendships don't just happen. Friendships require emotional intelligence, vulnerability and hard work. We need to be alert when friends are upset, angry, jealous, or simply need to be left alone. We need to be good listeners, practice the laying on of ears.

Touch is important in friendships. A simple touch on the arm is more likely to evoke a positive response. President Bush was well-briefed about touching the Crown Prince. Unhappily, it's bad manners for the English to touch each other.

Friend-making and friendship-keeping have become survival skills. Modern society encourages more of us to live alone, apart from a network of close family and relatives. Living alone, we may suffer a kind of psychological anorexia, deprived of the nourishment of friendships. Away from family, our friends can become like kin. Just watch TV sitcoms like Friends or Sex and the City. We seem designed to thrive in small social groups. Especially in later life, a strong network of friends promotes health and longevity. Loners are twice as likely to die from all causes.

Friendships between women involve disclosure and support. Male friendships usually mean shared activities. Overhear American conversations between women at lunch: they're talking about people, feelings and relationships. At a nearby table of men, they're talking about money, sports and sex. The women share their vulnerability. The men compete. They women may cry a bit, but leave refreshed. The men may leave still bleeding inside. Same gender friends are important, of course. Yet both sexes find friendships with women the most rewarding. Why? Women seem to work at their friendships, and it shows. Men, well ... it's something to do.

Friendship is both art and skill. Friendship is a cornerstone of human happiness. Look through those Holiday cards one more time. Work on those important friendships before the Holidays roll around again.

Charlie and I were close friends for thirty years. He regularly called us at home between 5 PM and 6 PM on Christmas Eve, when only close friends' calls would be welcome. Charlie died several years ago. This past Christmas Eve, I emailed Charlie's children telling them how much we miss Charlie and his Christmas Eve calls.

Close friends die, but their friendships survive. In the words of lyricist Stephen Sondheim, "They die but they don't."

30

Happy Families: Self-Mediation Skills

Discord is a fact of family life.

Mediators can help resolve current disagreements and prepare families to manage their future differences. Successful dispute resolution, present or future, relies largely upon the family's own self-mediation skills.

Family discord doesn't necessarily mean the family is unhappy. Nor does relief from current discord necessarily restore them to happiness. And this makes me uneasy. I worry that resolving the current dispute isn't enough. Without improving their self-mediation skills, the family may slip back into old patterns of stuck hostility.

Similar concerns gave birth to positive psychology ten years ago. Positive psychologists fashioned a "happiness-misery index" ranging from +5 (bliss) down to -5 (despair). They worried that as people undergoing therapy became less miserable—and approached zero on the happiness-misery index—they might slip backwards into old miseries. Without some positive guidance, they might not understand how to negotiate the happiness index north of zero. Positive psychology was conceived to help guide that exploration.

Unfortunately, the positive psychologists haven't yet offered very much about family happiness. They haven't yet tested novelist Leo Tolstoy's famous dictum, "All happy families resemble one another, but each unhappy family is unhappy in its own way." However, positive psychologists offer one very valuable clue: the happiest people are those who are intimately and positively engaged with other people. A family can be both training facility and primary arena for happy engagement with others.

My mediation experience is mostly with once happy families whose disagreements about money or business has left them stuck. Or at least they are unhappy about what divides them. It's not the money that divides them … at least not altogether. Their relational estate is the family's most valuable non-financial asset—that complex stew of genes, history, heritage and relationships that connects them across generations. The source of family discord lies somewhere inside their relational estate. That's also where you'll find their self-mediation skills, such as they are. The mediator's primary task is to activate and supplement those latent self-mediation skills.

Some self-mediation skills are those that created the family wealth: intelligence, energy, shrewdness, boldness, tenacity, imagination. Too often, however, equally important self-mediation skills are left underdeveloped or neglected, such as:

- habits of comfortable communication;

- maintaining clear boundaries between personal independence and family interdependence;

- rivalry and jealousy management;

- accepting differences;

- a capacity to differentiate between thinking and feeling, and a vocabulary for both;

- a willingness to forgive;

- healthy emotional engagement;

- listening without judging;

- encouraging individuals to speak their truth, but discouraging attempts to speak the truth of others.

Moneymaking and money spending have diverted family attention away from cultivating these vital skills.

The good news is that during mediation most families patch together sufficient self-mediation skills to resolve their immediate differences. Just barely enough. Too often it's an uncomfortably close call.

The past is powerful in families and they are slow to change. Without more, their self-mediation skills will subside and fall again into neglect. Without more, other differences will divide them and get them stuck later on. Without more, strife will remain imbedded in their relational estate. Without more, they will miss a golden opportunity to explore family happiness north of zero. The very self-mediation skills they neglect could be the keys to richer, happier family lives.

Mediators can help families identify the imbedded attitudes, patterns and practices that generate discord. Mediators can help families grow their self-mediating skills and thereby prevent, reduce or manage discord when it inevitably arises again. Confident that future discord won't undo them, once discordant families become free to explore the happiness territory north of zero.

In 1977, psychiatrist W. Robert Beavers (not a positive psychologist) published a scale describing five levels of family function. The Beavers Scale begins with the most dysfunctional family and moves up from worse to better.

- Level 5 families are chaotic and incoherent. There is no leadership; there are no rules. Misery abounds. There is no structure. Life makes no sense.

- Level 4 families are ruled by tyrants who control everyone. All is black-and-white. The tyrant's rules are inflexible. There is no room to negotiate. The tyrant dictates not only proper behavior but how everyone should feel.

- Level 3 families are rule-bound but have no tyrants. Rules are considered necessary because human beings are uncaring and untrustworthy. The rules are invisible referees, both internal and external. Spontaneity is suspect.

Beavers doesn't define "happy families" as such, though families functioning at Levels 3, 4, and 5 would have a hard time with happiness. Conversely, families at Levels 1 and 2 seem to interact largely north of zero.

- Level 2 families are relationally healthy. They are comfortable with loving feelings as well as feelings of annoyance and frustration. They respond flexibly to life's events. They focus on tasks with clarity. There is conflict but it can be resolved. They may disagree but they trust each other. Because their fundamental relationships are secure, they can work out differences without threatening their relational web. Differences are enriching. Everyone has adequate space. Being oneself doesn't betray the group. Intimacy feels safe.

- Level 1 families are quite similar to Level 2 families, just more competent, especially more egalitarian.

The Beavers Scale is the descriptor of family functionality most used by psychotherapists today. I doubt that Beavers intended to create rigid pigeon holes to classify every family. I prefer to think he described points along a continuum. In my experience, I often observe attributes on several Beaver levels in a single family. There may be tyranny but it's not absolute; there's chaos, but not always; there's rule-bending and ignoring rules at times; in certain circumstances an otherwise dysfunctional family can behave quite competently on Level 1.

Perhaps soon, positive psychologists will provide their own scale of family function along with strategies for upward mobility on a family happiness-misery scale. Meanwhile, mediators will work to engage and improve self-mediating skills.

Comfortable communication, non-judgmental listening, speaking for oneself but not for others, emotional engagement, rivalry management, separated thinking and feeling, willingness to forgive, accepting differences—these are not just self-mediation skills. They are relational guideposts to family enrichment and fun north of zero, gate passes to Level 2 or even Level 1.

With these self-mediating skills at work in their relational estates, perhaps happy families do resemble each other, as Tolstoy observed.

Part Five

Detecting and Defusing Potential Flashpoints

Some Guideposts and Warning Signs:

54. The optimum time to settle family disputes is *before* the lawsuit is filed.

55. Most families who find themselves in litigation thought it would never happen, or hoped so.

56. Most families in litigation claim they were shocked that relatives would sue them. They didn't see it coming. They didn't detect the "flashpoints" that triggered the lawsuit.

57. The first step towards avoiding family wealth litigation is early detection of the sources of discord—the "flashpoints" that generate the dispute.

58. If there are "flashpoints" in your relational estate, and family members respond candidly to the Flashpoint Detector Questionnaire, you will spot sources of potential discord.

31

Flashpoint Detector

There is an alarming increase lawsuits dealing with family wealth. These legal "Doomsday Machines" are proliferating, ripping and tearing precious family relationships built up over generations of patient nurturing. Our family mediation firm is dedicated to keeping families out of court. So far, we have been extraordinarily successful.

The optimum time to settle family disputes is *before* the lawsuit is filed. The most effective safeguard is prevention of discord, or at least sensible management of family differences. Most families who find themselves in litigation thought it would never happen, or hoped so. Most claim they were shocked that a relative would sue them. They didn't see it coming. They didn't detect the "flashpoints" that triggered the lawsuit. Now they feel blind-sided, betrayed.

The first step towards avoiding family wealth litigation is early detection of the sources of discord—the "flashpoints" that generate the dispute. On the following pages you will find a "Flashpoint Detector" questionnaire. If there are "flashpoints" in your relational estate, and family members respond candidly to this questionnaire, you will spot sources of potential discord in your family.

The Flashpoint Detector builds on the creative work and long experience of John and Malane Spears of Decatur, GA a husband and wife lawyers specializing estate and fiduciary litigation.

The Flashpoint Detector is designed to alert your attorneys and other advisors to potential flashpoints. Ask them to review your family's responses to the Flashpoint Detector.

FLASHPOINT DETECTOR QUESTIONNAIRE

This questionnaire is designed to detect situations, circumstances, persons or relationships called "flashpoints". Flashpoints could generate future disputes, claims, or litigation involving your estate plan. We strongly suggest that you review the results with your attorneys and other advisors.

We acknowledge the contributions of fiduciary litigators John and Malane Spears of Decatur, Georgia, whose originality and experience is reflected throughout this questionnaire.

COLUMN I:

Enter your answers under Column "I" to the left of the question.

> If your answer to the question is "<u>yes</u>" enter <u>2</u>
> If your answer is "<u>no</u>" enter <u>0</u>
> If you <u>don't know</u>, enter <u>1</u>.

Don't attempt to explain or qualify your answers.

As used in these questions:

- the word "*fiduciary*" means any executor, trustee or guardian who may serve under your estate plan, or another's estate plan, at any time.

- the word "*beneficiary*" means any person or organization who may receive a gift or bequest under your estate plan, or someone else's estate plan, at any time.

- the word "*estate plan*" means any gifts to any beneficiary at any time during your lifetime and after your death.

- the words "*family*" and "*family member*" means your relatives by blood, by marriage or by adoption.

I	II	III	IV		
—	—	—	—	1.	Are there any important facts or estate planning decisions that cannot be shared with your spouse or significant other?
—	—	—	—	2.	Do you consider yourself to be in good health?
—	—	—	—	3.	Are you insurable?
—	—	—	—	4.	Are any of your immediate family members or beneficiaries of your estate: handicapped, in poor health, recipients of SSI or Medicaid or in any way in need of special planning and protection?
—	—	—	—	5.	Do any of your family members or other intended beneficiaries have substance abuse, addictions, or similar special problems?
—	—	—	—	6.	Are you currently involved in litigation?
—	—	—	—	7.	Do you anticipate being involved in litigation?
—	—	—	—	8.	Are there any unwritten understandings with family members or other regarding your estate?
—	—	—	—	9.	Are there unresolved conflicts or hard feelings that would make it difficult for any of your fiduciaries to serve?
—	—	—	—	10.	Is there any unusual factor, anticipated problem, or dispute that you expect to arise at the time of your death?
—	—	—	—	11.	Are you in poor physical or mental health?
—	—	—	—	12.	Have you or members of your family been involved in guardianship proceedings?
—	—	—	—	13.	Do you serve as a fiduciary for any beneficiary of your estate, or of any other estate?
—	—	—	—	14.	Does any beneficiary of your estate serve as a fiduciary for your benefit?
—	—	—	—	15.	Do you have a confidential relationship with any beneficiary of your estate?
—	—	—	—	16.	Have you been married previously?
—	—	—	—	17.	Are there children of your previous marriages?
—	—	—	—	18.	Has your spouse been married previously?

I	II	III	IV		
—	—	—	—	19.	Does your spouse have children of previous marriages?
—	—	—	—	20.	Are you alienated or estranged from any of your children, or from any of your spouse's children?
—	—	—	—	21.	Is your spouse alienated or estranged from any of his or her children, or from any of your children?
—	—	—	—	22.	Are you or any of your beneficiaries living with, or closely involved with a partner to whom they are not married?
—	—	—	—	23.	Do you have close companions or close personal caretakers to whom you are not married?
—	—	—	—	24.	Are you the personal caretaker of another person to whom you are not married?
—	—	—	—	25.	Is there any significant undisclosed information in your family that, disclosed or not, could have a significant bearing on your estate?
—	—	—	—	26.	Are there significant unresolved disputes in your family or among your beneficiaries, longstanding disagreements or hostilities, or family members or beneficiaries who do not speak to each other?
—	—	—	—	27.	Do you have a joint account or joint property ownership with any other person?
—	—	—	—	28.	Does your estate plan create joint ownership or joint control of any significant assets?
—	—	—	—	29.	Does any family member or beneficiary of your estate have an unrealistically high or unreasonably low estimation of your wealth, or the value of his or her share of your estate?
—	—	—	—	30.	Will any family member or beneficiary of your estate be significantly disappointed or offended with his or her share of your estate?
—	—	—	—	31.	Does any family member or beneficiary have an unrealistically high or low expectation of what he or she will receive from your estate?
—	—	—	—	32.	Are there sufficient assets in your estate to carry out your estate plan?

I	II	III	IV		
__	__	__	__	33.	Are there assets in your estate that would be difficult to divide among two or more of your beneficiaries, such as works of art jewelry, or vacation homes.
__	__	__	__	34.	Are there assets in your estate that would be difficult for your beneficiaries to share, e.g. vacation homes, works of art, or jewelry?
__	__	__	__	35.	Do any of your beneficiaries perceive any promises agreements, entitlements, or understandings regarding your estate?
__	__	__	__	36.	Are there any "hidden agendas" between you and members of your family, between you and your beneficiaries, or among your beneficiaries such as righting past inequities, imbalances, wrongs, hurts, or injustices?
__	__	__	__	37.	Does your estate plan make non-traditional gifts, such as gifts to pets, housekeepers, unrelated friends or others who do not ordinarily benefit from estates?
__	__	__	__	38.	Does your current estate plan deviate significantly from your past estate plans, such as changing shares received by beneficiaries, introducing new beneficiaries i.e. your new spouse, or omitting beneficiaries who were formerly included?
__	__	__	__	39.	Does your estate plan create potential conflicts of interest among your beneficiaries? Some of these conflicting interests could be creation of a life estate, income and remainder beneficiaries, etc.
__	__	__	__	40.	Have you made any unstated assumptions about human nature that your beneficiaries may not share, e.g. "I know they will be fair", "I know they will cooperate", "we will never divorce", "my spouse will never remarry."
__	__	__	__	41.	Does your estate plan undertake to affect beneficiaries' conduct after your death, e.g. giving, withholding, or controlling money or property conditioned on a beneficiary's behavior?
__	__	__	__	42.	Does your will or other estate planning document criticize or unfavorably characterize any beneficiary or person close to him or her?

I	*II*	*III*	*IV*		
—	—	—	—	43.	Are any of your beneficiaries difficult people? For example, is any chronically angry, combative, litigious, dissatisfied, meddlesome, highly controlling, extremely opinionated, naïve in business or personal matters, or unwittingly inept?
—	—	—	—	44.	Is there any fiduciary appointed in your estate plan who may: decline to serve, who lacks the temperament or will to be firm with your beneficiaries, who lacks expertise, who has a history of acrimony with any beneficiary, or who has a conflict of interest with any beneficiary?
—	—	—	—	45.	Are there persons other than family members or beneficiaries whose influence could precipitate a dispute, claim, or lawsuit about your estate plan?
—	—	—	—	46.	Do you anticipate that there will be future litigation arising out of your estate plan?
—	—	—	—	47.	Do you have children other than those named in your will or estate planning documents?
—	—	—	—	48.	Is there the possibility that you will have or adopt more children?
—	—	—	—	49.	Do you have children born out of wedlock?
—	—	—	—	50.	Is there a possibility that you will be involved in an unresolved paternity claim?
—	—	—	—	51.	Do you have, or care for children informally placed for adoption?

COLUMN II:

Imagine that your adult family members, and all other living adults who are beneficiaries of your estate plan, are meeting together <u>today</u>.

You give each person a list of the above questions and propose a group discussion of each question, one by one.

- If you and that group of persons could *productively* discuss that question *today*, then it is a "green flag" question.

- If an attempt to discuss that question *today* would not be productive—i.e. it would provoke stony silence, anger, intemperate argument, yelling, crying, or someone might stomp out of the room and slam the door, then it is a "red flag" question.

- If you aren't certain whether the group's response *today* would be "green flag" or "red flag", then it's a "yellow flag" question.

In the space to the left each question, under Column II indicate how productively your adult family members and other adult beneficiaries could discuss that question together *today*:

- Write a "<u>G</u>" if "green flag",

- Write an "<u>R</u>" if "red flag", or

- Write a "<u>Y</u>" if "yellow flag".

COLUMN III:

Please review each of the questions again. Identify those "flashpoints" that are most likely to generate a dispute, claim, or litigation regarding your estate.

This time, identify *up to five* questions that spot "flashpoints" likely to cause trouble.

Under Column III to the left of each question:

- Write a "1" beside the question that describes the *most likely* situation to cause future difficulties,

- Write a "2" beside the second most likely,

- Write a "3" beside the next most likely,

- and so on to "5".

If there are *more than five*, you may list up to ten.

COLUMN IV:

Column IV seeks to identify those potential "flashpoints" that could be reduced or minimized by addressing them or attempting to manage them *currently*.

This time, review only those questions (five or perhaps up to ten) that you have marked in Column III above as likely to cause trouble.

Which of those potential "flashpoints" might be alleviated, minimized or at least managed by action taken *currently?*

Now, under Column IV to the left of the question, and in order of importance to the ultimate success of your estate plan, list those potential "flashpoints" you identified in Column III that could be made better, or at least less disruptive, by current action:

- Write an "A" for most important to the ultimate success of your estate plan,

- Place a "B" for second most important,

- Place a "C" for next, and so on to "E", and

- If you list more than five, continue down the alphabet.

Part Six

Organizing Healthier Wealthy Families

Some Guideposts and Warning Signs:

59. *"Noses in, fingers out"!* That's the most important advice I have for directors, whether they serve on the board of a public company, a family business, or a local charity.

60. Plunder-parasite boards, composed of inside and outside shareholders, are cluttered with misplaced noses and fingers.

61. An owner-manager badly needs the benefit of the rich business experience, good judgment and all-important vision that only good *outside* directors can supply.

62. Adding wise outside directors can transform the board room from battlefield to level playing field for both plunderers and parasites, and usually realigns noses and fingers.

63. To a considerable extent, a wealthy family is already organized around its financial wealth. But that's not enough. Your family organization should include your relational estate.

64. A family council is a systematic approach to share family information and news, to seek or give family advice, and sometimes to make family decisions.

65. Where a wise family council sets the rules of the road and synchronizes the lights, it can be a great ride. Where families and wealth intersect, collisions

and traffic jams can and do occur. A family council can minimize the hazards.

66. Experiment with a family council. Over time your family flag can change hues: from orange, to yellow, to a lime green which is probably good enough.

67. Beginning with a test drive, your family council can become a habit, a custom, a tradition, and eventually part of the heritage imbedded in your relational estate.

68. Too much estate planning for married couples focuses unduly on "when both of us are gone" with too little attention paid to the twenty years or so that the widows of this world ordinarily survive their husbands.

69. Too much attention is paid to transferring financial wealth and avoiding taxes, while too little attention is given to the relational estate, where wealthy families *live*.

70. Professional advisors need to inquire not only about client finances and health care arrangements, but also about flashpoints that might disrupt family peace and how clients wish to be remembered to their dear ones. In short, they need to provide *relational estate planning*.

32

Lessons from Geese:
Interdependence

1. As each bird flaps its wings, it creates an "uplift" for the bird following. By flying in a "V" formation, the whole flock adds 71% greater flying range than if the bird flew alone.

Lesson: People who share a common direction and sense of community can get where they are going quicker and easier because they are traveling on the thrust of one another.

2. Whenever a goose falls out of formation, it suddenly feels the drag and resistance of trying to fly alone, and quickly gets back into formation to take advantage of the "lifting power" of the bird immediately in front.

Lesson: If we have as much sense as a goose, we will stay in formation with those who are headed where we want to go, and be willing to accept their help as well as give ours to the others.

3. When the lead goose gets tired, it rotates back into the formation and another goose flies at the point position.

Lesson: It pays to take turns doing the hard tasks and sharing leadership—with people, as with geese, we are interdependent on each other.

4. The geese in formation honk from behind to encourage those up front to keep up their speed.

Lesson: We need to make sure our honking from behind is encouraging—and not something else.

5.   When a goose gets sick or wounded or shot down, two geese drop out of formation and follow it down to help and protect it. They stay with it until it is able to fly again or dies. Then they launch out on their own, with another formation, or catch up with the flock.

Lesson: If we have as much sense as geese, we too will stand by each other in difficult times as well as when we are strong.

That's interdependence.

For each family member, the relational estate contains the scales upon which the balance is struck between interdependence and independence.

33

Advice for boards of directors: Noses in, fingers out.

"Noses in, fingers out"! That's the most important advice I have for directors, whether they serve on the board of a public company, a small business, or a local charity.

In business corporations, the shareholders elect directors to represent them on the board. Good directors should have sophisticated business experience, good judgment and vision. Wise directors keep their noses in: do their homework, ask searching questions, listen carefully, and challenge management in constructive ways.

Directors choose a chief executive officer to manage the company day-to-day. Wise directors tell the CEO where they want the company to go, and hold the CEO accountable for getting there. They don't try to tell managers how to do their job. That would be micromanagement—fingers in. Wise directors keep their fingers out of management.

The interaction of this three-tier system—shareholders, board of directors, and management—is called corporate governance. In some public companies, governance isn't working very well. Directors tend to be the rich, the famous, the politically well-connected, and CEOs of other public companies. Look closely: those CEOs are probably directors on each others' boards. As a result, directors of poorly governed public companies eat the plate that management sets before them—noses out. And now and then, Enron happens.

But suppose it's a small family corporation. The owner-shareholder is also the CEO. Who needs a board of directors to hold an owner-manager accountable to the owner-shareholder, if they're the same person? On paper there's a board, of course. Every corporation must have one, most likely the owner, his or her spouse, and a trusted employee. If this board meets at all, it's to pass resolutions required by the bank, or real estate transactions, or the company's retirement plan. Everyone votes and signs as the owner directs. No one, including the owner, really noses in.

With fingers in everything, and so close to day-to-day problems, an owner-manager can lose perspective, detachment, and objectivity. An owner-manager badly needs the benefit of the rich business experience, good judgment and all-important vision that only good *outside* directors can supply. "Outside" means directors who are outside the family, outside the company, and outside the circle of people who can't afford to disagree with the owner. Only true outsiders can truly nose in.

Suppose several family members own the shares. Some work inside the company, others don't. Outsiders suspect insiders of plundering the company through excessive compensation, hidden perks and other deviousness. Insiders view outsiders as parasites who demand excessive dividends, too generous with advice and criticism, and too stingy with appreciation and gratitude.

Plunderer-parasite board meetings are cluttered with misplaced noses and fingers. In the fray, the board loses valuable perspective, detachment and objectivity. The fractious board badly needs the rich business experience, judgment and all-important vision that only good outside directors can supply. Adding wise outside directors can transform the board room from battlefield to level playing field for both plunderers and parasites, and usually realigns noses and fingers.

"Noses in, fingers out" is especially important for board members of churches, schools, charities and other non-profit organizations. Too often, there's a shortage of knowledgeable noses on non-profit boards. Too often non-profits select their directors from among financial contributors, eager volunteers, and the socially skilled and influential, with too little regard for business experience, judgment, or vision. However well-intended, this produces a finger board that may be more hindrance than help to a worthy cause.

"Noses in, fingers out" applies as well to managers. Most of your subordinates can do their jobs. They expect you to tell them what to do, but resent your telling them how to do it.

34

Organizing the Relational Estate: Forming a Family Council

I began this book by discussing the "relational estate", any family's most valuable non-financial asset. A relational estate is genes, history and heritage and a web of relationships that connect family members across generations. Just as the family financial estate requires careful management, so does the relational estate. A family council organizes the relational estate, linking family dynamics to family wealth.

Business and financial wealth are already scrupulously organized. Too often, however, the relational estate is not.

Absent a will, intestacy laws divide one's property according to the presumed intention of deceased persons, as determined by the lawmakers. There's no such tidy default provision for relational estates. Neglected relational estates invite trouble.

Some business families have enjoyed highly organized relational estates for generations. Theirs are models for us. If your business family is looking for a starting place to organize, here are some threshold suggestions. Consider a family council.

A family council is not just a family shareholders' meeting, or an occasional family reunion, or a family gathering in response to crisis, though a family council could accommodate each of these. A family council is a systematic approach to share family information and news (both business and personal), to seek or to give family advice, and sometimes to make family decisions. Rarely is a family council a legal entity. It doesn't supplant or overrule existing boards of directors, fiduciaries, or managers, but rather informs their judgment through thoughtful and organized family input.

The family council may suggest, but rarely directs. On occasion, it articulates family preferences or provides "a sense of the family". In rare instances, it may decide highly sensitive issues, e.g. should a family member be discharged from family employment? Should the name of a family company be changed? Should the family name be invoked in a public promotion?

Necessarily, a family council decides who may participate in its deliberations—who is "family" and who is not. Are collateral aunts, uncles and cousins included in the family council, along with spouses, widows and widowers, fiancées, non-marital partners or non-marital children?

How does the family support and nurture its members: children, teenagers, the elderly, those who are sick and disabled, addicted, geographically separated, alienated, detached or disinterested? How does the family encourage education and self-improvement, a sense of vocation, career planning, the work ethic?

How does the family relate to its wealth? Is there family consensus about inheritance, distributions, dependency, entitlement, investment, spending, saving, leisure, recreation? How does the family nurture its enterprises by promoting leadership development, orderly succession, meaningful family employment subject to appropriate entry rules?

How does the family relate to the community through philanthropy and community service? How are its charities and causes selected? How does the family promote its public image, yet protect personal privacy and personal safety? Who speaks to the public or the media on behalf of the family, and what is said?

How does the family relate to its advisors, to its key employees, and its fiduciaries? How are family disputes discouraged, prevented, or managed? When they arise, how are disputes resolved?

How, when and where does the family council convene? How does it preserve and promote family stories, family history, family heritage, family ethical, moral, religious or spiritual values? How does it encourage family members to keep in touch, become better acquainted, to enjoy each other, to have fun together?

I suggest a few preliminary meetings to try out the process. Expand natural family gatherings: tack on a day or two after your annual shareholders' meeting, or extend a holiday. Choose a resort setting or other meeting site that's emotionally neutral. Bring the little ones; provide child care and children's activities. Schedule no more than a half-day for meetings. Prepare and distribute an agenda in advance; invite input from all. Circulate news and information items beforehand.

Create an atmosphere of comfortable and safe discussion. Encourage participants to speak their minds respectfully. Discourage attempts to speak others' minds. Listen without judging. Be patient and helpful to those not familiar with financial statements or business practices. Express appreciation to your business leaders.

Eventually, write down in a Family Charter the plan of organization for your family council, your procedures, your family's basic values and family vision. Revisit your Family Charter often. Revise it when circumstances change, and at least once each generation.

I work at the intersection of family enterprise and the family's relational traffic. Where a wise family council sets the rules of the road and synchronizes the lights, it can be a great ride. Where families and wealth intersect, collisions and traffic jams can and do occur. A family council can minimize the hazards.

35

Queen Ellen's Family Council

A Genogram helps us visualize a relational estate. A Genogram of Ellen's family on the front cover of this book will help you follow this story.

Ellen is her family's *chief emotional officer*. She's the first to know of a family need, the first to offer help. She is generous with her money and her time, but cautious with her advice. Ellen is in her mid-seventies. She and Hugh had been married fifty-two years when he died four years ago. They had four children.

Ellen relishes her role as the queen of family gatherings. She is alert and carefully attuned to family interactions. She's painfully aware of the sharp words sometimes exchanged. Sometimes she intervenes, but mostly holds back, allowing her quiet queenly presence to cool tempers and blunt insults. More than they realize or admit, the family counts on Ellen to keep the peace.

Ellen never shares family unpleasantness with outsiders, and only rarely with her advisors. Voicing deep maternal hope, she insists, "I know they will be fair. I know they will cooperate". Ellen desperately wants her family to get along but worries that they won't, without her to keep the lid on family discontents.

Ellen is very private about her finances. Only her oldest son, Robert, knows the extent and value of her property. But she has not discussed her estate plan with him. Sharing her late husband's concern that significant inheritance would create problems in the family, Ellen plans to give the bulk of her own estate (separate from Hugh's estate) to charity. This may surprise family members because she has not been particularly philanthropic in the past.

Robert

Ellen's eldest son Robert, 54, is intelligent, strong and supportive like his father, whom he resembles. Robert bought the family company from his father's estate.

Ellen assumes that Robert paid a "rock bottom" price for the shares, their value as reported on Hugh's estate tax return. She worries that the other children will view this low purchase price as favoritism. In retrospect, Robert believes he paid an excessive price. The company's profitability has declined under his management.

Robert signed installment notes for the purchase price. Those notes are held by Ellen's marital trust and are several payments in arrears because the company is struggling. Ellen is the trustee but has said nothing to Robert about the past due installments.

The two adult children of Robert's failed first marriage have rejected his family. Though Ellen helped finance their educations and still sends them periodic gifts and cards, they never thanked her. They never call or contact her, or Robert, or any other family member to Ellen's knowledge. Ellen can't avoid feeling hurt.

On the other hand, Robert's second marriage seems happy and durable. His second wife, half a generation younger than he, has young children from a prior marriage whom Robert has not adopted because their father won't consent. Ellen has genuinely welcomed these step-grandchildren into the family and contributes to their educations. They seem sincerely attentive and thoughtful towards Ellen. But she's not sure what, if anything, these step-grandchildren should receive from her estate.

Mildred

Mildred, 52, married Walter against her parents' strong objections. Nevertheless, Ellen once quietly gave Walter a sizable sum of money for a business venture. It failed. Ellen considered the money a loan, but Walter has not mentioned repayment, nor has Ellen. Robert learned of this transaction while reviewing Ellen's tax returns but has said nothing. Walter has since obtained his PhD, which Ellen helped finance, and now teaches at a small college.

The couple's only child is learning disabled and will require moderate lifetime care. Mildred is overwhelmed by the child's needs and depressed by Walter's unavailability. Mildred and her brother Robert have always been close. Mildred was very supportive during Robert's divorce. Mildred depends on Robert for financial advice. This irks Walter who considers Robert intrusive, even controlling.

To Robert, Walter is a financially naïve academic lost in his books. You or I might speculate that Robert overplays his role as oldest brother, particularly since his father's death.

Ruth

Ruth, 41, the family superstar, is a highly successful pediatric neurosurgeon. Ellen and Hugh supported Ruth during her extensive medical training, but lost track of the high cost. Ruth lives with her lesbian partner of many years. The partner has one child, whom the couple planned, and whom Ruth has adopted. From outward appearances, Ruth, her partner and their child are accepted as part of the family, though Ellen suspects others may have deep reservations. It's always awkward when the partner and child arrive at family gatherings while Ruth is still at the hospital. Ellen thinks she has made peace with Ruth's orientation and lifestyle. Still, she wonders if she would feel differently towards the child if her daughter Ruth were the birth mother.

Jeff

Jeff, 39, is an adventurer whose current goal is to climb the principal peaks on all seven continents. He is handsome, winsome, even dashing. His spellbinding adventure stories are the high point of the few family gatherings he attends. Jeff's nieces and nephews adore him, as do a number of women around the world.

The family erroneously assumes that Ellen supports Jeff, though she hasn't given him money since college. Robert and Jeff speak only at family gatherings, and then superficially, often sarcastically. Robert disdains Jeff's lifestyle as irresponsible and wasteful. Jeff resents and rejects Robert's unwarranted assumption of their father's role in the family.

Wealth and Health

A significant portion of the family wealth passed at Hugh's death into various trusts. Ellen receives most of the trust income for life. That income permits Ellen to live as she chooses. What she doesn't spend is building up her own estate. Her current will leaves everything by roots to her children. However, Ellen is considering some significant lifetime charitable giving from her own funds.

Hugh's trusts give Ellen the power to reallocate trust assets as she sees fit among their children and grandchildren. She can exercise that power to reallocate only in her will, not during her lifetime.

Ellen is in good health. Her parents lived into their mid-nineties. Ellen's life expectancy is plus or minus twenty years. As Ellen inevitably declines over the next twenty years: will her judgment be impaired? Might she be subject to undue influence from family members? How will her health decisions be made?

Flashpoints

Her attorney worries about flashpoints of potential family discord as Ellen ages. Gnawing at him is her hollow affirmation: "I know they will be fair. I know they will treat each other right". Her words have an uncertain ring, more motherly aspiration than realistic expectation.

According to Robert, Hugh's last years of business leadership were complicated by failing health and rigid ways of doing things. The family company was in decline when Robert bought it from the estate. Robert has since attended the Owner-President-Manager Program at the Harvard Business School and is busily building a new company culture. Ellen's lawyer gently reminded Robert that he isn't allowed to finance this corporate reengineering out of delayed payments on his purchase money notes. Robert seemed to understand.

Ellen is most concerned about Mildred's learning impaired child. She has been asked to make a sizeable contribution to the child's school. When asked about plans for the child's lifetime care, Ellen mechanically recited a duty to treat all her children equally. The lawyer reminded her that Hugh's will empowers her to treat her children *un*equally—to make disproportionate distributions to their children and grandchildren from his estate.

When asked about her grown grandchildren by Robert's first marriage, tears gathered as she answered. Robert's ex-wife has asked Ellen for a large sum of money to finance drug rehabilitation for their son. Asked if any family member is in touch with Robert's children, Ellen confided that her younger son, Jeff, has a regular e-mail correspondence with Robert's daughter, an outdoor enthusiast. They regularly exchange digital photos and family news. Jeff knows about his nephew's needs for drug treatment.

With genuine misgivings, Ellen's lawyer launched a flashpoints discussion. Should Ellen identify flashpoints, there might be little he could do to help. She might deny her flashpoints, or admit them but choose to do nothing. Or she might rely too heavily on his advice. How to begin the flashpoint conversation?

"Ellen, suppose the family were to name you Queen for Life and Peacemaker Emeritus?

"I *am* the Queen … but who would keep the peace?

"A 'parliament' would keep the Queen's peace. You could form a family council."

"Say more. I worry that our family will just drift apart when I'm gone."

"Your influence may keep the lid on some potential flashpoints but postpone some very important conversations that need to happen while you are still the reigning Queen."

"*What* flashpoints?"

"Here's my flashpoint list, Ellen:

- Robert's overdue notes;
- how other family members would react to Robert's overdue notes if they knew about them;
- Robert's success or failure in your former family business, even though the family no longer owns it;
- Walter's unpaid 'loan' for his failed business venture;
- the varied circumstances of your grandchildren, e.g.

  - Robert's alienated children
  - His addicted son
  - Robert's attentive stepchildren
  - Mildred's challenged child
  - Ruth's adopted child;

- the tensions between Robert and Jeff;
- your unannounced charitable intentions beginning with your gift to the school for Mildred's child;
- your children's widely varying income and financial needs;
- how you will leave your own estate;

- how you might reallocate Hugh's estate among your children and grand-children."

Ellen stands, walks to a window, gazes silently for a long moment:

"… I see."

"Ellen, I hope your family will leave the door unlocked for Robert's children to return some day."

"I can't help my mixed feelings. I may pay for his drug rehabilitation. That could be my way back to him."

"I suspect that Hugh is very present at your family gatherings?"

"The children were very hurt by Hugh's death, still grieving I suppose…. They die but they don't."

"Wealthy families are joined at the wallet."

"Yes, and I'm not comfortable holding the family 'wallet', especially Robert's notes. Robert doesn't discuss his personal finances with me. I know that Mildred and Walter are very dependent upon her trust distributions. Ruth certainly doesn't need the money … and could care less. I have no idea how Jeff finances his mountain adventures."

"Your family council will need to discuss money. I hope your family can talk openly and frankly about how money matters to them, and why."

"We've mostly 'talked around' money, even when Hugh was living. I think money distances us … pushes us apart.

"Distance from family deprives individuals of support from their relational estate that simply cannot be supplied by other relationships."

"Our family is both close and distant. We sound close when we're together, but it often feels distant. I think they're trying too hard to protect the Queen from unpleasantness."

"So, 'Please the Queen' is a form of peacekeeping? Is everyone playing that game … including you, Ellen?"

Stung, anger rising, Ellen glared at her lawyer. But after pondering his question, she softened:

"You may have a point. How could a family council keep the peace?".

"Distance from family magnifies differences, promotes alienation even invites litigation. Not talking about important things distances families. Avoiding, pretending, denying. Silence is terribly ambiguous. Silence can mean anything. We assume the worst from silence."

"But if we talk, we might fight. There are raw feelings lying just below the surface."

"It could be edgy at times. But suppose your family continues the way it is until you are gone. What then?"

"I see … well, how would we start this?"

"Why not let the family know that the Queen would be very pleased if they would take a serious look at a family council?"

"If I abdicate as peacemaker …" Ellen sputtered. "Do families *really* talk about their flashpoints?

"Some do. Others just pout, or fret, or shout or sue. A family feud is a terrible thing."

First Steps

Ellen's family experimented with a family council. At a family gathering they took a test drive, with awkward fits and starts at first. More than once Ellen had to step down from the Queen's throne and become Margaret Thatcher for a time to keep the family council moving forward without jumping the tracks. Sometimes she felt like a single mother of four rebellious adolescents. Particularly wrenching was the session during which the family exchanged their responses to the Flashpoint Detector questionnaire. "It's not fair to Mom! If we go on like this, we'll all be in court some day!"

After a second test drive, and a third, the family began to buy in to the process. *We support what we help create.* Over time the family flag changed hues: from orange, to yellow, to a lime green where it remains today. They don't function at optimal Level 1 on the Beaver scale, but for Ellen's family, lime green is good enough.

Ellen's family council became a unifying structure with a unifying process:

- for offering everyone a voice—including quiet Mildred;

- for listening without judging—Robert struggled with this;

- for exchanging information—but no further clues about Jeff's source of support;

- for asking and giving advice—about the family wealth, about distributions in particular;

- for making decisions—with more clarity, and after a few tears about Ellen's future health care decisions, building on Ruth's medical expertise;

- and, yes, for keeping the peace. Ellen eventually off-loaded most of her peace-keeping onto the next generation.

Beginning with a test drive, Ellen's family council became a habit, a custom, a tradition, and eventually part of their heritage imbedded in their relational estate. It is forum for serious family discussions about money and family relationships—the arena for self-mediation and the improvement of self-mediation skills.

Crisis Management

Crisis management in the White House is handled by special crisis teams whose members come from outside the White House staff. Involving White House staffers in crisis management would unduly interfere with their regular responsibilities. Their plates are already full. Special crisis management teams don't wait until a crisis occurs to get organized. They work together on non-critical projects: pool their skills to build the team before a real crisis confronts them.

For more than twenty years, I have mediated family crises about family wealth and family business. Unlike the White House, my client families can't delegate crisis management to outsiders. They must do their own work. Yet in the midst of crisis, most client families discover that, when coupled with the mediator's skills, they *do* have the self-mediating skills, as a family, to meet their crises ... if barely.

Some of those self-mediating skills are the very business skills that created their wealth: intelligence, energy, shrewdness, boldness, tenacity, imagination. However, equally important self-mediating skills have been neglected, underdeveloped, such as:

- habits of comfortable communication;

- clear boundaries between personal independence and family interdependence;

- rivalry management;

- accepting differences;

- a capacity to differentiate between thinking and feeling, and a vocabulary for both;

- a willingness to forgive;

- healthy emotional engagement;

- a family that listens without judging;

- that encourages individuals to speak their truth, but discourages attempts to speak the truth of others.

Moneymaking and money spending have diverted family attention away from cultivating these critical self-mediating skills.

The good news is that most families can catch up on neglected family skills … again … if barely. As Ellen's family discovered, self-mediation skills can be learned and taught, and eventually absorbed into the relational estate as a part of family heritage.

Three words best describe the dramatically altered relational estate that evolved out of their family council: *Ellen's ultimate legacy.* And it all started when a wise lawyer took a chance by challenging a wealthy widow: "Ellen, suppose your family were to name you Queen for Life and Peacekeeper Emeritus?"

A Plea

Too much estate planning for married couples focuses unduly on "when both of us are gone", with too little attention paid to the twenty years or so that the Ellens of this world will survive their husbands. Too much attention is paid to transferring wealth and avoiding taxes, while too little attention is given to the relational estate, where wealthy families *live.* Scant attention is paid to people, relationships and circumstances that could ignite flashpoints later on.

In an earlier chapter, I wrote about poor King Lear and how his crazy estate plan—land for flattery—created the aging king's worst nightmare. Poor Lear died penniless, his health destroyed, his family a train wreck, demented and conversing with mice, forever immortalized by Shakespeare as one of history's great tragic fools.

Beginning in their sixties, increasingly in their seventies, and quite certainly in their eighties, these are what all aging persons want and need these most:

1.   Financial security

2.   Attentive health care

3.   Peace in the family and

4.   To be remembered lovingly and favorably.

Professional advisors need to inquire not only about client finances and health care arrangements but also about flashpoints that might disrupt family peace and how clients wish to be remembered to their dear ones. In short, they need to provide *relational estate planning*.

By not settling for the role of aging Queen, by anticipating the potential flashpoints that might survive her, by insisting on formation of a family council to contain the smoldering flashpoints, Ellen will be remembered by her children and grandchildren as generous, wise, deeply caring and tough loving.

Ellen will have left her children not only wealth, but a functioning "good enough" relational estate … which is priceless.

Appendix A

Reprinted with permission. This article appeared in the Fall 2004 issue of the *ACTEC Journal*; 30 ACTEC Jr. 150.

Organizing Wealthy Families Around Value and Vision:
Creating a Family Council
by Gerald Le Van

How does a wealthy family make the most of being "joined at the wallet" for successive generations?

How is privilege best leveraged?

This article was prompted by James E. Hughes Jr., "Family Wealth—Keeping It in the Family", (Bloomberg Press, 2004). Jay Hughes, now retired, was a highly successful sixth-generation lawyer specializing in international financial transactions, when he found himself "lost in a dark wood", as Dante (and Hughes) describe mid-life crisis. After a year of extensive reading and thought, he refocused on helping families make the most of their wealth.

Hughes is a thoughtful writer about families and money, an engaging personality and personal friend. Though he focuses on old money with a New Yorker's slant, Hughes has much of importance to say to any wealthy family. His writing is ebullient and wordy, peppered with frequent references to the classics and to his own family's experience.

Below, I have summarized some of his principal points. You or I may not agree with Hughes on specific issues. At times he portrays a wealthy family as though it were an investment portfolio, referring to family members "human capital" and to cumulative family knowledge and wisdom "intellectual capital". He writes at length about the incorporation of family value and vision into a representative form of family governance. I wish he had said more about how to accomplish that. I wish he said much more about family interactions, family relationships and family systems.

Nevertheless, Hughes proposes a broad and positive agenda that's worth thoughtful family consideration, especially for those who are forming a family council.

1. A family's primary wealth consists of *human capital* (its members), and *intellectual capital* (everything each members knows and the family's collective knowledge); *financial capital* (its fortune) is secondary.

2. A family's greatest wealth is human capital—the individual human beings who form the family.

3. Growing human capital is the family's primary responsibility.

4. Growing human capital is the surest way to preserve family financial wealth.

5. A family can successfully preserve human capital over a long period of time.

6. Successful long-term preservation of wealth requires a system of *governance* (joint decision-making) that results in slightly more positive decisions than negative ones, over a period of at least one hundred years.

7. Family governance must be reenergized in each generation in order to overcome entropy.

8. The dark concept, "shirtsleeves to shirtsleeves in three generations" is recognized in many cultures. The first generation generates the wealth (*creativity*), the second generation preserves it (*stasis*), and the third generation dissipates it (*entropy*).

9. Wealth preservation is a dynamic process, not a static process.

10. Long-term wealth preservation (100 years or more) contemplates at least four generations.

11. In family wealth preservation time horizons: "short term" is twenty years; "mid-term" is fifty years; and "long term" is one hundred years.

12. Whether or not they own or control an operating company, a wealthy family is a family business.

13. The fundamental issues of wealth preservation are *not quantitative*. They are *qualitative* issues of human and intellectual capital.

14. Most families fail to tell the family stories that bind them together and make them unique.

15. Most families fail to understand that preservation of wealth over a long time horizon is very hard work with high risks of failure and reward.

16. A family should form a written *family compact* among its members that expresses their shared *vision* and *values*. Each successive generation should reexamine, reaffirm, and readopt that family compact.

17. To enhance its human capital, a family should:

    a. Stretch the capacities of each family member to achieve his or her maximum well being.

    b. Insure that every member's basic requirements for food, clothing and shelter are met, including emergency care.

    c. Insure that every member attains his or her highest educational limit and his or her highest role in family governance.

    d. Emphasize the dignity of work as a basic requirement of individual self-worth, and help each family member find the work that enhances self-worth and individual happiness.

    e. Encourage geographical diversification of family members throughout the world.

    f. Encourage, recognize and practice family spiritual values as contained in the family compact, as expressed in family governance and family philanthropy.

    g. Enhance family intellectual capital—the collective knowledge of all family members.

h.   Provide clear information on all family governance matters and seek feedback

i.   Provide incentives for the family's highest achievers to take leadership roles in family governance.

j.   Provide tools to younger members to learn family stories and prepare for later roles in family governance.

k.   Stretch the intellectual capacity of each family member to achieve his or her highest level of learning.

l.   Diversify intellectual capital by encouraging study of world cultures and languages.

18. Suggestions for preparing a family compact.

a.   Include rules for conducting family meetings.

b.   For the first meeting, ask each family member to prepare a detailed personal resume describing the personal talents, aptitudes and training that he or she can make available to family enhancement and family governance.

c.   Ask each family member to write down the ten values most crucial to the family's long-term success.

d.   Ask each member to imagine him or her looking back from age 105; write down what he or she would tell immediate family members had been most important.

e.   Ask each member to write a description of the family twenty years hence.

f.   Ask a small committee writes a brief family history.

g.   Create a representative family government.

19. Consider these family rituals to be instituted and observed:

a.   Coming of age

b.   Creation of a new family "elder"

c.   Arrival of a new member by birth, marriage, etc.

d.   Death of a family member

e.   Introduction of new outsider members—non-family advisors, mentors, etc.

20. The family should keep "balance sheets" and "income statements" on human capital and intellectual capital.

21. The family should allocate financial investments to creation and growth of human and intellectual capital.

22. The family should leverage family capital growth through a *family bank* that makes appropriate loans that may be too high risk for commercial lenders, but low risk to the family because the proceeds would be used to preserve family wealth by financing enhancement of human and intellectual capital. Such loans would bear reasonable interest and require repayment.

23. Family governance should keep close tabs on family advisors, protectors, mentors, fiduciaries etc.

24. The family should teach and mentor its members on the roles and responsibilities of excellent beneficiaries.

25. The family should monitor all fiduciaries of family wealth regarding their administration, investment and distribution of family wealth.

26. Philanthropy is the family's *social capital.* It is a means for family members, isolated by wealth, to connect with larger issues of the world and find a place in it.

27. Family philanthropy involves the giving of human and intellectual capital as well as financial capital.

28. The family should periodically evaluate each member's progress towards the family vision as contained in the family compact. The evaluation should address:

a.   Is the person free or dependent?

b.   Is the person self-aware?

c.   Has the person sought searched for a vocation? If so, is he or she pursuing it? If not, why not?

d. Does the person perceive the difference between work as calling and work as wages?

e. Does the person have a mentor in pursing a calling? If not, does he or she have the skills to find a mentor?

f. Does the person have the humility to apprentice in order to become proficient in a calling?

g. Does the person understand the difference between hubris and humility, and the consequences of each towards personal happiness?

h. Does this person have friends? Who is he or she towards those friends?

i. Can this person express love?

j. Can this person express compassion for himself or herself and others?

k. Can this person express gratitude?

l. Can this person express joy and humor?

m. Does this person have a view of what is true, good, beautiful, just and right?

n. Can this person balance justice with mercy?

o. Does this person perceive the difference between courage and bullying?

p. Does this person take active roles in the larger civil society? In stewarding and giving to others?

q. In which of the above areas is this person competent, and in which are areas of growth required?

29. As to family financial capital, periodic inquiry might ask:

a. Does he or she have an excellent facility for choosing advisors and mentors?

b. Does the person understand risk and reward?

c. Does the person understand stewardship in the context of preserving family wealth?

d. Does the person understand the reciprocal obligations of drawing on and investing in family financial capital?

e. Does she or he work to instill financial knowledge in the next generation?

f. Does the person participate in family governance by undertaking life-long learning about dynamic wealth preservation?

g. Does the person actively seek competence and eventual excellence as a beneficiary, limited partner, shareholder or owner, as a member of family boards (for profit and non-profit), and in other financial relationships with the family?

30. Does the family engage in periodic *peer review* of its fiduciaries?

31. Has the family considered creation of a *private trust company* to handle its fiduciary requirements?

32. Uncles and aunts can be important guides and mentors to younger family members, at times accomplishing what parents cannot.

33. True mentoring is the mentor's expression of wisdom through intuition in guiding another towards greater self-awareness and the pursuit of happiness. Mentoring is neither teaching, nor coaching, nor being a best friend, nor being an elder. Mentoring is about asking questions, not giving answers. Successful mentoring is dialogue in which both parties learn something essential. Ideally, a trustee will function as mentor to the beneficiaries.

34. Elders tell and retell the family stories. Elders remind the family of its history, its values and its vision. They advise on matters in family disputes. Where necessary, elders function as the judicial branch of the family. They deal with family disputes, resolve them, and if necessary, enforce their decisions.

35. Creating perpetual ("dynasty") trusts should be undertaken only after sober consideration of its non-tax implications on future generations.

Jay Hughes' provocative book caused me to rethink some of my own views about organizing wealthy families.

1. The family is our fundamental human relationship. Our families bore us, raised us, nurtured us, taught us, supported us, loved us, disciplined us, educated us, and challenge us. We share common genes and a unique history.

We are the story we tell each other without speaking. Our unique stories bind us together.

2. Family is a fundamental need.

3. We cannot leave our families, even if we rarely see each other or never speak.

4. We continue to share family with those who have died.

5. Our family is a tether to our history, our genes, and to ourselves. Without family, we would be as lost as an astronaut on a space walk whose tether has parted, doomed to fatal drift.

6. A family's greatest wealth is its members. Their nurture, growth, development, welfare, well-being and happiness are the family's chief responsibilities and its surest way to preserve financial wealth long term.

7. Wealthy families are joined at the wallet. Shared wealth forces them either closer together than families not so privileged, or else farther apart.

8. Distance from family deprives individuals of non-financial support and resources that cannot be supplied by other relationships. Distance from family magnifies differences. Distance from family promotes alienation and invites litigation.

9. Closeness compels wealthy families to organize.

10. A Family Counsel formalizes family organization.

11. Organizing a Family Council only around the wealth overlooks other compelling family needs and rich family resources.

12. Organizing a Family Council around family vision and value can maximize all family resources, including wealth.

13. Begin family organization by identifying value—what is ultimately important to the family? Admit that wealth is important. Now what else? Write down what you mean by family value.

14. Once value is identified, move on to vision. What will this family be like in 100 years if we do nothing? What might this family become in 100 years if

we commit to a greater vision of ourselves and our descendants? Write down your family vision.

15. Once vision and value are identified, organize your getting together. Who convenes us, where, how often? Who is invited? Organize play time and catching up time, as well as work time. Write down how you plan to convene in the future.

16. Once your Family Council is convened, what's the agenda and who prepares it? Who will have agenda input? Will it be distributed in advance? Write down your agenda procedures.

17. What information do we share as a family? Business? Financial? Family news? Good news and bad? Do we limit our discussions to information sharing? Write down what types of information the Family Council should circulate while together and apart.

18. Do we invite outsiders to report or give advice? Can we bring our own advisors? Write down your rules about inviting guests and advisors to family meetings.

19. Does our Family Council make recommendations or requests to family fiduciaries, to managers of family companies, to individual family members or family groups? Do we give advisory opinions on matters affecting the family or family wealth? Do we make decisions? Write down what your family is authorized to do while it meets together.

20. Who will lead deliberations at Family Council meetings? What are their duties and responsibilities? Write them down.

21. Who will lead the family in the interim between meetings? To what extent do our leaders speak and act on behalf of the family when we aren't convened? How should leaders keep the family informed of pending decisions? What may they say or do with and without prior notice to the family or family approval? Write down what you expect from family leaders between family meetings.

22. On actions to be taken by the family, who votes? How are votes counted? Must all agree? Does a simple majority rule? Or is a larger majority on highly important matters? Write down your voting rules.

23. If we disagree or can't seem to decide, how will we resolve opposing positions? Write down your family dispute resolution process.

24. Combine your written vision, values, rules and procedures into a Family Charter, then follow it.

Some additional thoughts about Family Council organization:

- There should be a written charter.

- The family may want to consider adopting a Code of Conduct for family behavior.

- How votes are counted can produce fascinating discussions and tense moments, e.g. one person one vote or by family or ownership groupings.

- The Charter can require that no legal action can be commenced against trustees, or officers or directors of the family company without prior Family Council review.

- List other matters that need to be considered first by Family Council to prevent "end runs" by family members via Trustees, Management, etc.

- Provide specifically for the use of trust or company assets, e.g. planes, recreational facilities, club memberships, for lending the family name to companies and causes.

- Watch especially for hidden or unequal perks and other perceptions of favoritism.

- Carefully and systematically disclose all compensation and perks received by family members from the trust or company. Encourage recipients to disclose voluntarily, rather being coerced to reveal compensation and perks.

- Discretionary dividends and trust distributions are always delicate. Should there be Family Council input to persons exercising discretion?

- Consider ownership disparities among family groups. Some younger generation members come into their money before others.

- Conversations about how other relatives spend their inherited money are seldom productive.

- Consider a rule that no advisors for individual beneficiaries may attend meetings unless invited by Family Council.

- Sometimes, company activities carry unintended but clear intimations of family support. The family may or may not want to be identified with:

  - Company philanthropy

  - Company activism

  - Company paternalism—benefits, work rules, retention and discharge, downsizing

  - Company compliance, e.g. environmental, ADA, sexual harassment.

- The Family Council can take a role in preserving family heritage. Few families lose their curiosity or concerns about their history, roots, identity, genetics, etc. No matter how remote their control over ownership of the trust or company, they continue to ask:

  - "Who am I?"

  - "Who are we?"

  - "How much of us is preserved in company archives, mementos, photos, minutes, etc?"

  - Public image and reputation are always important to business families. "It isn't the money ... altogether."

  - Sensitize trustees and company management to family sensitivities, e.g. name, image.

  - Sensitize the family to trustee and company stresses, loyalties, frustrations, regulations, and particularly public company disclosures.

  - Agenda suggestions for Family Councils:

    - spend time on family news

    - invite input from all family, company management, and trustees

    - emphasize *learning and understanding*.

    - make allowance for *different levels* of business sophistication, business judgment, interest in the Company, and attention spans.

    - Trustee representation: how much do representatives of corporate trustees really contribute?

- Family representation: be careful about "lines", classes of stock, generations, custom and tradition.

- Management representation: who besides the CEO really needs to be a director?

- Appoint at least three active *independent* outside directors, who are neither family, employees, or otherwise beholden to Family, Management, or Trustees.

- Family co-trustees or trust advisors

  - For all of the trusts? For those only in co-trustee's bloodline?

  - For trusts for one's own benefit as learning experience?

APPENDIX B

Reprinted with permission. This article appeared in the July 2006 issue of Estate Planning, a publication of Thomson Tax & Accounting; 33 Est. Plan. 20 (July 2006).

BUSINESS PLANNING
Business Succession Planning That Meets the Owner's Needs

By enhancing one's capacities as a counselor, the estate planner has an extraordinary opportunity to serve the family of clients who are business owners and to ensure the family's financial and emotional well-being over several generations.

Author: DANIEL H. MARKSTEIN, III, ATTORNEY

DANIEL H. MARKSTEIN, III is a shareholder in the law firm of Maynard, Cooper & Gale, P.C., which has offices in Birmingham and Montgomery, Alabama. He is President-Elect of the American College of Trust and Estate Counsel and a Fellow of the American College of Tax Counsel. Mr. Markstein has lectured and written extensively on estate planning.

According to the Small Business Administration, 90% of the 21 million U.S. businesses are family-owned, and one-third of the Fortune 500 are either family-owned or family-controlled. Yet only 30% of family-run companies succeed into the second generation, and a meager 15% survive into the third.

In the face of all the political oratory and criticism of the "death tax" that gave us the Economic Growth and Tax Relief Reconciliation Act of 2001 ("EGTRRA") and that has resulted in the current attempt permanently to repeal the transfer tax, in over 35 years of practice I have never observed a family business that had to be sold in order to pay estate taxes. On the other hand, I have observed several instances in which family businesses had to be sold because business acumen cannot be transmitted genetically. In short, in my experience, family businesses have been sold typically because the founder or his descendants decided to grasp the opportunity to take advantage of a liquidity event, family disharmony made it necessary for there to be a liquidity event, or the ineptitude or lack of commitment (or both) of succeeding generations made it necessary to dispose of a family business before it withered away in voluntary liquidation or bankruptcy.

Yet even where businesses have been successfully transferred to succeeding generations, by accident or design, it is the exception rather than the rule that formal succession planning is undertaken and implemented, with appropriate assistance from qualified professionals, at a time when such activity can make a difference in the outcome. In some cases, there has been a member of the family who was the obvious successor; in some cases, there has been competition that has been either healthy and productive or unhealthy and destructive; and in some cases, it has been obvious that successor management must come from outside the family.

As Amy Braden has observed, "Being the owner of a plane doesn't mean you have the right to fly it, and being the pilot doesn't mean you can decide which routes to fly." [1] In other words, ownership succession is different from management succession. We proceed on the assumption that the best approach is to begin the process of business succession planning when the principal owner or owners are still in their 50s and are at the peak of their powers. The questions are what is the best approach, given the particular family circumstances, and how to effect implementation of the process that is decided upon.

Background

As I have observed estate plans come to fruition, I have worried that we have failed to help prepare the next generation or generations for the challenges and opportunities that they will confront. The issue is more transitional than transactional, and that issue will remain whether or not the estate tax is repealed. The attorney must be prepared to be the counselor, the trusted advisor, rather than merely the tax expert and/or the drafter. He or she must be ready to venture beyond the boundary of a narrow specialty and help families address the human and emotional issues that are often exacerbated by significant wealth.

A recent study found that only half of family-owned businesses had succession plans and of those about 50% were created by lawyers, 19% were created by the owners themselves, 15% were created by accountants, and the remaining 16% were created by a variety of other advisors and consultants. [2] In many cases, the focus of advisors and commentators is retaining the role of quarterback. [3] Other advisors and commentators who are specialists in transfer tax law limit the succession planning discussion to transfer tax rules. [4]

Much of what we know about business succession planning involving family businesses has been gleaned from newspaper articles or courts' opinions involving prominent families such as the Pritzkers, the Dolans, the Ambanis, the Thyssen-Bornemiszas, the Herzes, the Binghams, the Hafts, the Murdocks, and others. In addition, albeit rarely, we obtain anecdotal information from those families who overcome their penchant for privacy to speak to reporters. [5] Although it has been observed that the Pritzker family convinced themselves of the great fallacy that a few people at the center can take care of all the problems of a family business, an Alabama entrepreneur who is chief executive officer of his family business spoke to a reporter and admitted at age 68 and after a liver transplant that "I want to continue as long as I can." [6]

One commentator suggests organizing a nine-member team that includes an accountant, a business appraiser, a financial planner, a psychologist, a banker, an insurance agent, a broker, an actuary, and an attorney. [7] This is reminiscent of the old saw that a camel is a horse designed by committee. Still another extreme suggestion is to closet family members with one or more mediators in an extensive multi-day retreat. [8]

Another commentator who is experienced in counseling family businesses expressed the point of view that, "if you protect the viability of the business, matters seem to work out." [9] He also made the following salutary suggestions:

• Keep in mind that this is an iterative process. Have patience....

• Do not sell the softer issues short. Remember, your client, her family members, and business team have never done this before. Be sure that all the relevant people are included in the process, erring on the side of completeness and inclusion.

- Try to get the client and the members of her system to identify their goals, core values, and beliefs.

- Many clients are geniuses at what they do but are not experienced in working with conceptual problems.

- The most important element in the larger transition process is the management succession plan. [10]

In advising clients, lawyers and accountants have exhibited tendencies to stick to what they know, focusing on the transfer and income tax aspects of business succession planning while giving short shrift to the emotional and relational issues that bind and sometimes confound members of families who are bound together by strands of DNA. Many professional advisors tend to shy away from these emotional issues. Many of them confront their clients in their offices and fail to take advantage of the opportunity—indeed the necessity—of getting on the ground, walking around the facilities of a family business with those in control, and obtaining a complete understanding of the dynamics of both the business and the family that controls it.

Almost two decades ago, Gerry LeVan, a lawyer who has become a family business consultant, noted estate planners' myopic preoccupation with documents and tax planning, and suggested that the passing of the family business to the next generation deserves more sensitivity on the part of estate planners and more willingness to seek expert assistance where needed. [11] LeVan was one of the first lawyers to suggest recognition of the necessary but temporary role of the family business consultant to serve as the facilitator and mediator who helps families resolve their futures and in doing so works himself out of a job. [12]

Byrle Abbin followed by reporting on the results of surveys of family business owners, who ranked the issues that confronted them in the following descending order of importance:

- Organizational structure of the business.

- Capable and supportive key management.

- Motivation of successors and management.

- Accommodation of family members.

- Estate planning.

- Retirement planning for current management.

- Retaining competent professional advisors.

- Operating with a board of outside directors. [13]

He also reported on another survey that noted the pervasive informality in approaching both the business and the business succession plan, the limited use of a wide circle of advisors outside the family, and the failure to use management tools that are common in public companies. [14]

LeVan's views are also echoed by Abbin's experience and conclusion that only once the "soft issues" have been addressed, assessed, and attended to, should the typical estate planner's bag of tricks be brought to bear. [15] That experience and conclusion leads him to recommend an approach that puts the family and business structure issues ahead of transfer tax and legal documentation and providing "holistic estate and succession planning" as the only logical and proper means of serving family business needs and providing solutions based on those needs. [16]

Some approaches to the process of planning

While an advisor or a business owner is considering a framework for the process of planning, practical reality dictates that business owners have estate plans. The preparation and implementation of the estate plan cannot be put on hold pending the completion of business succession planning. The business succession plan is a process that requires a considerable investment of time and the possible involvement of non-traditional professional assistance—i.e., the family business consultant. At the conclusion of that process, it is appropriate to revisit the estate plan. [17]

This process also requires that the attorney adopt the role of the counselor in assisting the owner to plan for the successful transition and transfer of a business. [18] In embracing the counselor role, both the attorney and the accountant must be cognizant of their obligations and limitations under applicable rules of ethics. [19] The introduction of a family business consultant, who is specifically trained in family business dynamics and family relations, can both improve the communications between family members in addressing family and business issues, and also overcome some of the ethical constraints that limit the abilities of attorneys and accountants to do so. [20]

Know your client

Abbin identifies and categorizes stereotypical basic entrepreneurs, and distinguishes them from technical entrepreneurs. He captures their personalities so clearly and well that his observations are set out at length below:

> The stereotypical entrepreneur has enormous ambition, energy and drive that manifests itself into an egotistical, compulsive, obsessive and impulsive nature. Often he or she possesses a mixture of stubbornness and arrogance and also may exhibit eccentricities. The basic entrepreneur is much more likely to exhibit intelligence than intellect, since focus is on intuition. Most have been rather successful in operating that way ... Thus, there is little or no system to the decision-making process. Lack of communication is endemic. Lack of teaching, and disinterest in detail, is commonplace in the operations under his approach.

> It follows from this that the entrepreneur does not engage in the classic sense. He leads and does at the same time. Confusion results from poor delegation, with all decisions typically flowing through him. Uncertainty is rife through exercise of a code of secrecy, so little or no information flows down from the entrepreneur, and as a result, little comes back up to him for empirical thought. Domination by him includes all family members, whether in or out of the business, as well as all key employees who essentially are "yes men or women." Thus, the typical entrepreneur is told whatever everyone expects he wants to hear, whether it relates to reality or not. ***

> Inherent also is the entrepreneur's sexist attitude about the business acumen of daughters and the likelihood that, although the best in abilities, a daughter will be overlooked in favor of the less competent sibling-son. The history of family business is replete with the entrepreneur's domineering demeanor resulting in sons who lack the strength of their own convictions, obviously a self-fulfilling prophecy emanating from his activities as a patriarch, both of the family and the family business. Too frequently it includes his conclusion that the daughter married poorly and the son-in-law has to be taken care of, but has absolutely no abilities to provide input into the management of the company. Often this is an emotional conclusion devoid of any objective rationale. [21]

While the above described entrepreneur is dynastic, always wanting the family flag to fly high above the family business pole, that is not necessarily true of the "technical entrepreneur," whose goal

> is to build an enterprise, see it grow and prosper, gain financial independence or success, and ultimately "cash in on it" whether by an outright sale or going public. This type of entrepreneur has much weaker emotional ties to the business as it affects his personal attitudes and ego, let alone as it impacts family members, employees and business associates. ***

> It is evident that the "technical entrepreneur's" attitude toward their own children and business often is significantly different, since they have less emotionalism about continuing family ownership of the business. They more likely recognize that their children either are not interested in being successors in management or are not capable and perhaps should not be involved in the business because their own interests in life differ from that of the company. Making this decision about their children's capabilities, limitations and weaknesses appears to be much easier for the technical entrepreneur than for the general business entrepreneur. As a result, often their business succession plans do not consider having their children take over. This more cold-blooded attitude exhibits itself in a mindset that is much less dynastic, i.e., a commitment to keep the family business as a monument that often intrigues and drives the more typical business entrepreneur.

> Because the technical entrepreneur is more analytical by nature and training, there is a greater likelihood he or she would be interested in implementing better business procedures. Their business organizations tend to be better organized and on a less intuitive basis than that of the older style business entrepreneur. [22]

Even so, personality studies show that controlling entrepreneurs, the risk-takers with capital, are primarily concerned about minimizing risk. That accounts, at least in part, for their guarding control and their having difficulty in trusting their best employees or their children. In the second generation, it appears that sibling groups are even more risk-averse than the founder was. Their mantra is to avoid losing their inheritance as opposed to building a legacy for future generations. Succeeding generations may have a greater challenge because they have had no appropriate role models for collective ownership. Thus, the success of those who wish to transfer stewardship and a sense of legacy to succeeding generations has been possible only because "both the generation in charge and the successors were willing to do the hard work of hashing out administrative issues, redefining their mission and designing new structures to serve the broadening and diversifying family." [23]

The Family Office Exchange has identified and categorized the risks to affluent families and their businesses as follows: business ownership and control, investment concentration, ownership structures, fiduciary exposure, financial oversight, family office, family and philanthropic legacy, and intra-family relationships. It is a difficult challenge to motivate family members to discuss risks and to adopt a process for managing them. Participants in the Family Office Exchange's 2005 "Thought Leaders Roundtable" proposed a six-step framework for family risk management: (1) define the family's objectives for its wealth, (2) identify the risks that threaten those objectives, (3) prioritize those risks according to likelihood of occurrence and level of impact, (4) create mitigation or contingency plans for the most critical risks, (5) commit resources to oversee the mitigation plans, and (6) continuously monitor the family situation and environment to update the risk management plan. [24]

How may the chances of success be enhanced? One family business consultant, Earnest Doud, suggests that it is critical to recognize that the answers that worked for the last generation may not be the right answers for the next generation. [25] He has developed a framework for effective succession planning that involves a six-transition model:

1. *The founder's (current leader's) transition.* The founder must have a clear sense of personal direction for the future; become a good teacher, mentor and door opener; and have financial resources independent of the operating results of the business.

2. *The family transition.* To achieve the goals of business prosperity, family harmony, and personal well-being, adult family members must have the ability and willingness openly to confront issues that may have a high emotional content.

3. *The business transition.* To achieve operating efficiency, change must be embraced where it is indicated, and management teams must be strengthened. The family must define and abide by the rules by which it will manage both the family and the business relationship. In addition, a strategic

vision is necessary to achieve the discipline of participating in systematic strategic thinking.

4.   *The management transition.* A determination must be made as to whether a family member can succeed to the chief executive's position and, if so, he or she must be identified. If not, other options to family management must be considered. Competency and potential must be addressed objectively.

5.   *The ownership transition.* It must be determined who should have ownership and how to transfer ownership to the future owners in a manner that is both tax-effective and respectful of the needs of the business. In addition, a sense of responsibility must be inculcated into the family members who will succeed to ownership. Remember that fair is not equal and equal is not fair; the sooner that the ownership transfer decision is made, the more flexibility is available; and the sooner that the transfer occurs, the more tax-effective it can be, but the plan should not necessarily be tax-driven.

6.   *The estate transition.* While equal is not fair in the division of business ownership among family members, estate transfer decisions typically emphasize the family value of equality. Hence, the estate transition should follow decisions with respect to the ownership transition, which must ensure fairness and business continuity. An exit strategy is essential for those who do not participate in ownership of the business. [26]

Finally, Doud suggests that the following qualities are required to succeed in pursuing the framework described above:

- Vision: knowing what the family stands for.

- Values: knowing what the family stands on.

- Voice: having and using the ability to communicate effectively.

- Vehicles: designing the mechanisms by which to implement decisions.

- Viability: knowing whether the required financial, management, and personal resources are available or are able to be developed when needed.

- Volition: commitment and guts. [27]

Jay Hughes, a distinguished lawyer and counselor to family businesses learned from his father that businesses rarely failed due to a failure of their financial practices, but rather they most often fail because of poor long-term succession planning. [28] Hughes suggests that the proverb "Shirt sleeves to shirt sleeves in three generations" (or its Chinese and Irish analogs, "Rice patty to rice patty in three generations," and "Clogs to clogs in three generations") results from a classic three-stage process of business development: a period of creativity, a period of stasis, and a period of decay. [29]

Hughes observes some of the reasons why those proverbs come true in some cases:

1.   Wealth preservation has connoted wealth measured as financial capital. Few families have understood that their wealth consists not only of financial capital but also of human and intellectual capital; and "Even fewer families have understood that, without preservation of their human and intellectual capital, they cannot preserve their financial capital."

2.   "Families fail to understand that the preservation of their wealth is a dynamic, not a static, process and that each generation of the family must be the first generation the wealth-creating generation."

3.   Families lack the discipline of patience and, therefore, fail properly to measure the time frame for successful wealth preservation. The result is that planning for the use of the family's human and intellectual capital is far too short-term and individual, and family goals for achievement are set far too low.

4.   "Families fail to comprehend and manage the external and internal liabilities on their family balance sheets." A family business that is trying to preserve wealth may be in a blissful state of status quo, but in fact what is developing is a state of entropy or decay because liabilities were not managed properly in the earlier stages of the family's lives.

5.   "Families fail to understand that the fundamental issues of wealth preservation are qualitative, not quantitative. Most families manage themselves to attain quantitative goals. These families measure success based on the size of their financial balance sheet … Unfortunately, this exercise omits the preparation and review of the family's and each individual member's qualitative balance sheets." Without a description and a valuation of a family's

and its individual members' human and intellectual capitals, the family and individual balance sheets are incomplete in measuring success in meeting the family's wealth preservation mission and goals. The following questions are critical in assessing whether a family is actively wealth preserving:

- Is each individual member thriving?

- Is the family social compact among the members of each generation providing an incentive to the leaders of each generation to stay in the family and to listen to the individual issues of those whom they lead so that the latter choose to follow?

- Do the individual family members know *how* to leave the family wealth management business so that they do not feel that they *have* to leave?

- "Are the selected representatives of the family meeting their responsibilities to manage the family's human, intellectual, and financial capital in order to achieve the individual pursuits of happiness of its members, and does each individual member perceive that they are doing so?"

6.   Families fail to tell the family's stories that relate the family's history and its values.

7.   "Families fail to understand that the preservation of family wealth over a long period of time is unbelievably hard work—with a tremendous risk of failure balanced by the highest possible reward. Most of us know that process is essential to the successful achievement to any endeavor. Most of us also know that leaving the process too soon, because it seems too hard, is the most common reason why the process fails. Families who choose to enter the process of long-term wealth preservation face the daunting fact that their process will never end if they are successful. They have to decide to stay in the process literally for all the generations to come." [30]

Other approaches to business succession planning

One answer to the question posed above of how families can be organized around a vision and values that includes both a summary of Hughes' points and a thoughtful reaction to them is offered by Gerald LeVan. [31] That response includes the organization and operation of a family council.

A family council is simply a meeting of multiple generations of family members that occurs regularly in order to educate family members and help them to make informed decisions on issues of interest to the family. [32] It creates its own rules of operation and, hopefully, adopts a mission statement and a values statement. It can provide linkage to the boards of family-controlled operating entities, it can provide a voice for non-active family members to express their views, and it can provide linkage to estate planning entities and structures. [33]

It is sometimes difficult for solution-oriented experts to avoid a rush to solution and instead acknowledge the importance of and embrace the concept of process. [34] The hardest step is the first one, for procrastination is the greatest risk not only to estate planning but also to business succession planning. In my experience, most entrepreneurs would rather address the issues in a business transaction, that might involve a minor part of the assets of the business, rather than address the problems of, much less engage in, estate planning and succession planning that involve essentially all that they have. The best weapons with which to attack procrastination are talent as a counselor and persistency.

Regardless of whether a family owns an operating business or whether the operating business has been sold and other assets have replaced it, family governance is important. In 2003, JPMorgan published an excellent portfolio entitled, "Effective Governance: The Eight Proactive Practices of Successful Families," in its *Challenges of Wealth* series. While the circulation of that portfolio was limited, recently the practices that are described in the portfolio were enumerated and elaborated upon in an article that is accessible easily to everyone. [35] The authors suggest that governance is important and that the issue is appropriately addressed by families when family members are committed to a collective identity (sharing a compelling economic and social reason for being connected), see themselves as stewards rather than owners, and are dedicated to empowering individuals. [36] The eight proactive practices of successful families are as follows:

1. Articulate a clear vision. This requires defining the company's mission and setting forth the values that guide the family in conducting the business or, when there is no business, the purpose of the family wealth.

2. Cultivate entrepreneurial strengths.

3. Plan ahead to reduce risk and act on opportunities.

4. Build unifying structures that connect family, assets, and community. This might involve a family constitution and a family council, as well as a family office, trusts, private investment funds, and philanthropic activities.

5. Clarify roles and responsibilities. It is important to distinguish between the responsibility of individuals as family members and their duties as asset owners or enterprise managers.

6. Communicate. This must be a studied activity rather than one left to chance.

7. Help individuals develop competencies. Doing so will foster individual fulfillment as well as family harmony.

8. Foster independence and provide exit options. [37] The ability to exit gracefully without recrimination should make a trip to the courthouse unnecessary.

Conclusion

By enhancing one's capacities as a counselor, the estate planning attorney has an extraordinary opportunity to serve the family of his or her clients and to ensure its financial and emotional well-being over several generations. Doing so may require some reorientation and some refinement of old skills as well as the acquisition of new ones. However, doing so is critically important in carrying out one's obligations; for, dressed up in whatever technical garb there may be, the problems that cross our desks are essentially the problems of human beings. In order to serve our clients well, we must understand the panoply of issues facing them and the waves of emotion on which they float, be prepared to help our clients deal with them, and never shrink from the tasks that our professional forbears confronted and our successors surely will confront, whether there are transfer tax considerations to take into account or not.

PRACTICE NOTES

The business succession plan is a process that requires a considerable investment of time and the possible involvement of non-traditional professional assistance—i.e., the family business consultant.

[1] "Preserving Family Harmony," JPMorgan Private Bank Portfolio, pp. 14, 18 (Fall 2005).

[2] Grove and Prince, "What, No Succession Plan?," 143 Tr. & Est. 69 (Sept. 2004).

[3] Coplan, Jones, and Painter, "Succession Planning for Wealthy Family Groups," 133 Tr. & Est. 31 (Nov. 1994); Dreux, Etkind, Godfrey, and Moshier, "Succession Planning and Exit Strategies for the High-Net-Worth Business Owner," 69 CPA J. 31 (Sept. 1999).

[4] Conway, "Current Issues in Business Succession Planning," 2003 Ohio ACTEC Meeting; Bourland, "When the Kids Won't Play Well Together: Tax-Free Corporate Divisions in Family Business Succession Planning," 38 *U. Miami Heckerling Inst. on Est. Plan.* Ch. 14 (2004); Bourland, "Implementation and Documentation of the Family Business Succession Plan," Univ. Tex. Sch. of L., Private Companies—Tools to Make Them Thrive (1/13–14/05); Hess and Haylik, "Attitude Adjustment," 144 Tr. & Est. 56 (Apr. 2005).

[5] Hazlett, "All in the Family," 143 Tr. & Est. 54 (Feb. 2004).

[6] *Id.* at pp. 55, 56.

[7] Basi, "Professionals in Business Succession Planning," ABA Tax Section 2001 mid-year meeting.

[8] Gage, Gromala, and Kops, "Holistic Estate Planning and Integrating Mediation in the Planning Process," 39 Real Prop., Prob. & Tr. J. 509, 538 (Fall 2004).

[9] See Dreux, et al., *supra* note 3, at p. 35.

[10] *Id.*

[11] Le Van, "Passing the Business to the Next Generation: Before Estate Planning Begins …," 14 Prob. Notes 257 (1987).

[12] Le Van, "Passing the Family Business to the Next Generation: Handling Conflict," 22. *U. Miami Heckerling Inst. on Est. Plan.* 1408 (1988).

[13] Abbin, "Here a GRAT ... There a GRAT—The Mass Merchandising of Estate Planning by Acronym—Planning for Family Business Succession Requires Much More," 29 *U. Miami Heckerling Inst. on Est. Plan.* 1103 (1995).

[14] *Id.* at 1105.3.

[15] *Id.* at 1114.

[16] *Id.* at 1126.

[17] Koren, "Preserving the Patriarch's Patrimony for the Prodigal and Other Paranormal (or Normal) Progeny: Non-Tax Considerations in Family Business Succession Planning," 31 *U. Miami Heckerling Inst. on Est. Plan.* Ch. 12 (1997).

[18] *Id.* at 1202.3; LeVan, "... and Counselor-At-Law," ACTEC ListServe (6/16/04).

[19] Koren, *supra* note 17, at 1205; Koren "Non-Tax Considerations in Family Business Succession Planning, Estate Planning for the Family Business Owner," pp. 17 et seq. (ALI-ABA, 8/1/02).

[20] Koren, *supra* note 17, at 1205.1F.

[21] Abbin, *supra* note 13, at 1108.1.

[22] *Id.* at 1108.2.

[23] Hamilton and Kaye, "High Net-Worth Families—Wealth Creators' Dilemma: How Much to Delegate?," 142 Tr. & Est. 42, 44–45 (May 2003).

[24] Hamilton and Nichols, "Eyes Wide Open," 144 Tr. & Est. 49 (Aug. 2005).

[25] Doud, "Challenges and Opportunities in Family Business Succession," 59 N.Y.U. Inst. on Fed. Tax'n §1401[2] (2001).

[26] *Id.*

[27] *Id.*

[28] Hughes, *Family Wealth: Keeping it in the Family*, p. 3 (1997).

[29] *Id.* at pp. 5 and 6.

[30] *Id.* at pp. 7–13.

[31] Le Van, "Organizing Wealthy Families Around Family Value and Vision," 30 ACTEC J. 150 (Fall 2004).

[32] Cohn, "They Lived Happily Ever After and Other Family Business Fairy Tales: Non-Tax Issues That Paralyze Succession and Estate Planning," 40 *U. Miami Heckerling Inst. on Est. Plan.* Ch. 11 (2006).

[33] *Id.*

[34] Brown and Rubin, "Attitude Adjustment," 143 Tr. & Est. 57 (Aug. 2004).

[35] Braden and Fisher, "After the Sale," 144 Tr. & Est. 63 (Apr. 2005).

[36] *Id.* at p. 64.

[37] *Id.* at pp. 64–67.

Acknowledgements

Some of these chapters originated as newspaper columns in the Asheville Citizen-Times.

Chapter 4, Sex, Money and Kids: Don't Create a Taboo

—Le Van, Raising Rich Kids (Xlibris 2003)

Chapter 7, Father and Sons: Their Unresolved Issues

—Le Van, Families Money and Trouble (Xlibris 2003)

Chapter 10, Litigation: The Family "Doomsday Machine"

—Quoted in Dukeminier & Johnson, Family Wealth Transactions, 2nd Edition Little, Brown & Co. 1978

Chapter 13, The "Soft Side" of Business: Clocks and Rain Forests

—Le Van, "Corralling the Soft Issues", Journal of Estate Planning, April-May 2001

Chapter 17, Parasites vs. Plunderers: Tensions Between Inside and Outside Shareholders

—Bingham, Passion and Prejudice: A Family Memoir (Applause Books 2000)

Chapter 22, Sibling-Shared Inheritances: Red Flags, Yellow Flags … or Green Flags?

—Edge, Robert G. "Children in a Rowboat and Other Potential Mistakes in Estate Planning", Probate and Property, January/February and March/April 2003.

—Le Van, Gerald "Healthy Wealth in Business Families" Business Entities, January-February 2000.

Chapter 24, Controlling Kids with Money: Incentive Trusts Rarely Work

—Le Van, op. cit.—"Trust Me, Baby: Heirs Meet "Incentive" Arrangements, Wall Street Journal, November 1999

Chapter 25, Happiness: A New Science?

—Time Magazine, January 17, 2005, pp. A1–A68.

—Layard, Richard, Happiness, (Penguin Press 2005).

Chapter 27, Pursuing Happiness: Why Not?

—"A Right, From the Start" Wall Street Journal, July 1, 2005, W11. McMahon is a professor of history at Florida State University. His new book, "Happiness: A History" (Atlantic Monthly Press 2005).

—In Jefferson's draft of the Declaration of Independence he wrote the phrase "pursuit of happiness" one time. No corrections or interlineations suggest he was searching for words. To view, go to:
http://lcweb2.loc.
gov/cgi-bin/ampage?collId=mtj1&fileName=mtj1page001.db&rec-Num=0544.

—According to Professor Seligman, each of us excels in three to five of these positive character traits. His VIA Signature Strengths Survey offers to measure these traits. It is available on his web site:
www.authentichappiness.com. Seligman's latest book is "Authentic Happiness: Using the New Positive Psychology to Realize Your Potential for lasting Fulfillment" (Free Press 2004).

Chapter 28, Happy Work: More Fun than Fun!

—See, Hoggard, "How to Be Happy" (BBC Books 2005) written to accompany a four-part TV series "Making Slough Happy" broadcast in November and December 2005. See Chapter 6, Happy at Work?

Chapter 29, Friendships: They Die But They Don't

—See, Hoggard, op. cit.—Chapter 4

Chapter 30, Happy Families: Self-Mediation Skills

—Beavers, W. Robert, MD, Psychotherapy and Growth: A Family System Perspective (Brummer/Mazel Inc. 1978)

—Tolstoy, Count Leo, Anna Karenina

Chapter 32, Lessons from Geese: Interdependence

—Milton Olson

978-0-595-44317-8
0-595-44317-6

Printed in the United States
143106LV00003B/58/A